Shaping Successful Junior Swimmers

DAVID WRIGHT

SHAPING SUCCESSFUL
JUNIOR SWIMMERS

BUILD A FOUNDATION. STREAMLINE YOUR TRAINING. CREATE WINNERS.

Meyer & Meyer Sport

British Library Cataloguing in Publication Data

A catalogue record for this book is available from the British Library

Shaping Successful Junior Swimmers

Maidenhead: Meyer & Meyer Sport (UK) Ltd., 2018

ISBN: 978-1-78255-140-9

© 2018 by Meyer & Meyer Sport (UK) Ltd.

Aachen, Auckland, Beirut, Cairo, Cape Town, Dubai, Hägendorf, Hong Kong, Indianapolis, Manila, New Delhi, Singapore, Sydney, Tehran, Vienna

Member of the World Sport Publishers' Association (WSPA)

Printed by C-M Books, Ann Arbor, MI, USA

ISBN: 978-1-78255-140-9

Email: info@m-m-sports.com

www.m-m-sports.com

CONTENTS

PREFACE

My intention, when writing this book, was to offer a practical guide to navigating the difficulties that can affect the transition years between promising junior and successful adult swimmer—difficulties that, if left unresolved, can result in early dropout from the sport.

But before getting into the subject of the book, I should tell you something about my coaching experience.

I was born on March 3, 1948, in the New Zealand Central Otago town of Lawrence. I attended Wairoa College in New Zealand, Thorp High School in Wisconsin in the United States and Victoria University of Wellington. I graduated with a BA degree in political science. And no, I still don't know why politics is called a science.

I am an American Swim Coaches Association (ASCA) International Level 5 swimming coach. I have coached national swimming representatives from New Zealand, the United States Virgin Islands, the United States of America and Saudi Arabia. Most notable students include NZ National, US State and Saudi Arabian Champions: Toni Jeffs, Nichola Chellingworth, Jane Copland Pavlovich, Joseph Skuba, Rhi Jeffrey, Jane Ip, John Foster, Lara van Egten, Loai Tashkandi, Eyad Masoud and Oswaldo Quevedo. In the case of Jane Copland Pavlovich and Nichola Chellingworth I was involved with their swimming from swim lessons through to national championships and international teams.

I was awarded the US Swimming's Certificate of Excellence in 2007, appointed as National Coach for the US Virgin Islands in 2003, coach of Toni Jeffs at the Barcelona Olympic Games and the 1992 World Cup Short Course Finals where she placed third, coach of Ozzie Quevedo in 2009 when he set two Masters World records in the 50 meters butterfly (24.15) and 100 meters butterfly (54.90), coach of Rhi Jeffrey when she qualified and swam in the 2012 USA Olympic Trials and in 2016 coach of Loai Tashkandi to two silver medals in Gulf Coast International Championships. I have just completed a coaching contract in Jeddah, Saudi Arabia, coaching an international team of Saudi swimmers.

In association with New Zealand track coach Arthur Lydiard and Jane Copland Pavlovich, I published two books on swimming: *Swim to the Top* in June 2002 and *Swimming—A Training Programme* in April 2004. I am a contributing writer to the swimming website www.swimwatch.net.

Prior to my career as a swimming coach, I coached track athletes including my wife Alison Wright, who represented New Zealand, Oceania and the United Kingdom over 800, 1500 and 3000 meters.

I have found it rewarding and educational to have guided competitors in the two principal Olympic sports of track and swimming to participate at Olympic and World Championship level in both sports. In coaching both swimmers and runners I have closely followed the principles and teachings of Arthur Lydiard.

Lydiard's training ideas were so obvious and simple, and they worked. I spent several years experimenting with the Lydiard programme. I ran 100 miles a week for 10 weeks and began to feel the adaptations that come from sound aerobic conditioning. I did not become an Olympic athlete but was convinced that both reading about and running a Lydiard programme had made me more than able to coach my wife, Alison, as a runner.

And I was wrong. In those early days, I made so many errors. It is a wonder Alison survived. I increased the build-up distance too quickly, and I reduced the anaerobic distance too much. I asked for speed sessions to be run too fast and set too much speed work. Alison's running suffered. Puzzled by what was going wrong, I contacted John Walker's coach, Arch Jelley, to see if he could help. Arch agreed. He did not change Alison's training. He still coached according to the principles Lydiard had developed 20 years before, but Arch understood the principles better than me and knew how to balance the programme, how speed fitted into anaerobic training and how anaerobic training fitted into a distance build-up. He understood the factors critical to coaching success. We all know the ingredients. Good coaches put them together properly.

Arch continued to coach Alison by correspondence. She became a national record holder over 1000 metres and national 1500-metre champion of the United Kingdom, Scotland and New Zealand and world ranked over 800, 1000, 1500 and 3000 metres.

Alison wins the Christchurch inter-primary school 100 yards on Lancaster Park where Peter Snell was about to set a world record for the 800 meters. Sometime later, Alison trains in Windsor Great Part. Note the well-known royal home, Windsor Castle, in the background. Our house was just through the fence on the left.

At the same time, Arch taught me that my knowledge of Lydiard's training was not enough. I did not understand how the pieces of the programme combined to produce a good result. Arch gave me that. This understanding of how to balance the programme was vital when I later began transferring Lydiard's methods from athletics into swimming.

Curiously, when I spoke to other swimming coaches, many of them supported the importance of a build-up, of background training and of aerobic conditioning, yet few of them balanced their training in the way Arch had instructed me it should be balanced. Many swimming coaches were still using interval-training methods and calling it a Lydiard aerobic programme. It seemed to me that many coaches were, and still are, making the mistakes I had made earlier with Alison's running training. Their programmes were not properly balanced, and young swimmers were being hurt in the process.

So when I started coaching swimming and wanted to convert Lydiard's principles from athletics to pool training, I knew I needed help. If getting the programme right had been difficult in athletics, I was aware that transferring it to a new sport was likely to present many problems.

I called Arthur Lydiard and began a telephone communication that took place each week, and sometimes each day, for eight years. Without it, converting Lydiard's principles to swimming would have been impossible; I would have lost my way.

Even with Lydiard's input, it took eight years to get the programme right. Hundreds of separate decisions had to be made. In each case, the physiological objective Arthur sought and his method of attaining it had to be translated to swimming. Running 100 miles a week achieved certain physiological changes in athletes—what was the swimming equivalent? Four weeks of anaerobic training was right for runners—was it right for swimmers? What was the swimming equivalent of hill bounding; could fartlek training be done in a swimming pool; did 30 minutes of anaerobic swimming have the same effect as 30 minutes of anaerobic running? What about Lydiard's views on weight training and stretching? Were they relevant to swimmers? What variations were needed for sprint, middle distance and distance swimming?

The conversion was not easy and without Lydiard it would have been impossible. It was an exciting time of discovery. The translation of even minor elements needed three or four adjustments, and each decision took a six-month season to test.

The keys to unlocking the secrets were Lydiard's availability and his willingness to solve the problems and my experience and knowledge of athletics training. We had a common understanding; We could communicate using the same language.

After eight years I felt I had resolved the fundamental questions. Swimming equivalents had been found for running around the Waitakere Ranges, for an easy run, for a hard eight lapper and so on. The basics were in place, and they were different—very different—and, for that reason, they were also very exciting.

The programme will require further fine-tuning. All training methods develop and adapt over time. But future refinements will accurately reflect Lydiard's principles. These are the foundations that have fashioned this swimming version of a sound, balanced training programme. A programme that, in large part, is essential in making certain junior swimmers survive.

INTRODUCTION

The purpose of this book is to discuss the factors that contribute to swimming's high dropout rate and to propose remedial measures that could improve the retention of junior swimmers. The following table is a one-page summary of the factors that coaches, parents, administrators and swimmers need to take into account; factors that will be discussed in detail in the book.

ACTION	EXPLANATION
Provide a balanced training programme.	This means supplying the three training inputs of aerobic, anaerobic and speed in a 40/20/40 ratio.
Understand and observe the differences between aerobic and anaerobic.	Many coaches set anaerobic schedules believing them to be aerobic. This causes harm and early dropout.
Treat team members as individuals in preparing training programmes.	Different team members react to training in different ways, which must be considered.
In young swimmers, focus on aerobic conditioning.	Physiologically this is the only type of training young swimmers can obtain any benefit from.
Restrict the input of anaerobic type training.	Junior swimmers should only swim anaerobic sets twice a week for a maximum of four weeks every six months.
Observe the importance of being fresh and sharp in the speed period.	When it is time to go fast, do not add to the physical stress by also increasing the volume of training.
Only swim 50 races in a six-month season; 100 races annually.	More than 100 races annually will likely cause symptoms of overtraining and early dropout.
Control and restrict the use of a stopwatch. Don't time everything.	Timing every speed set is unnecessary and adds to the likelihood of stress and early dropout.
Teach good technique using drills.	Good technique improves performance, and drills are an effective way of improving stroke efficiency.
Provide interesting lessons with a fun element.	Fun is a good way of holding interest and keeping swimmers involved in the sport.
Parents must show interest and support but can't be a second coach.	All sorts of problems arise when parents get too closely involved in the sport. There should be only one coach.
Don't push for early competitive results. Be patient.	For swimmers, coaches and parents, the importance of patience is paramount. Good things take time.
Study and apply good principles of rest and recovery.	Between seasons, sessions, sets and intervals, good training requires well-thought-out rest and recovery.
A coach is the means of travel, not the traveller.	The journey belongs to the swimmer. This is the best guide to the nature of the coach–swimmer relationship.
Encourage self-evaluation and discussion.	This is the earliest means of predicting initial signs of over training and the danger of early dropout
Use the Salo Pulse Plot as a predictive tool.	The test is the best physical means of predicting over training and the danger of early dropout.
When it is time to retire, have no regrets. Stay busy with a new activity.	Take heart; there is a good life outside of swimming. Stay busy, stay fit and enjoy.

CHAPTER 1

IS THERE A GLOBAL PROBLEM?

The short answer is yes. Around the world it is accepted that the dropout rate for swimmers between 12 and 18 years of age is between 70 and 80%. It is a staggering statistic. Every parent with a 12- or 13-year-old son or daughter involved in swimming knows that there is only a one in five chance of them still being involved in the sport when they reach 18.

Of course, as I said in my first book, *Swim to the Top*, there is nothing wrong with the dropout itself; it depends on the reasons for it. There is nothing wrong when swimmers retire because they have explored their talent or stop because other activities become more important. But if they stop before reaching their potential because they are exhausted, beaten and dissatisfied, then that is not good. It's not good because someone has done something wrong; it is seldom the swimmer's fault. They may be blamed, but the responsibility for their departure usually lies somewhere else.

In his book about New Zealand athletics, Peter Heidenstrom talked about Alison's running career and concluded by saying, "Alison is my favourite kind of athlete. In 1969, she was one of those television likes to call rubbish. It took her ten years, but she became one of the best in the world. As Shakespeare put it, 'We know what we are but know not what we might be.' Wright had the strength of character to stick at it and find out."

The primary purpose of all coaches should be to have the same comment made at the end of every swimmer's career, whether they retire as an Olympic medallist, a national finalist or as someone who just gave it their best shot. Anyone who has explored their potential share a common bond because they have had a common experience.

I have trained several swimmers who did not swim in the Olympic Games or win a national championship but retired just as successful. The best example was a swimmer from Auckland called Abigail Frink. She was tough, dedicated and conscientious. Season after season she swam weeks of 100 kilometres. She improved through Division II Championships, National Age Groups and finally swam a lifetime personal best of 34.76

to place third in the B final of the New Zealand Open Championships. Abigail knew she was working at the same level as Olympic champion, Rhi Jeffrey, but her ability was not the same. Abigail decided to retire, but not before she had explored her potential and had gone as far as she could go. She was as successful, as fulfilled, as any Olympic champion.

The teenage dropouts that are of concern are not the Abigails, but rather those who leave before exploring their limits. In Arthur Lydiard's book, *Running to the Top*, he said there were champions walking the streets of every town in the world. I agree with that. The talent of Nichola Chellingworth, Jane Copland Pavlovich, Rhi Jeffrey and Toni Jeffs is not unique to them. There are fine swimmers in New Zealand, Florida, the Virgin Islands and Saudi Arabia who should have swum as fast as those four swimmers but never did. They were talented enough; they toiled up and down swimming pools but never achieved their potential.

A few years ago, the great Australian swimmer Ian Thorpe was on a bus traveling in the south of France with Jane Copland Pavlovich. He asked Jane, "When I was younger I went to New Zealand to race. I was beaten by two guys. What happened to them?" Thorp mentioned their names. Jane had never heard of them. Makes you think doesn't it? Why did Thorp make it? Why did the two New Zealanders leave to do something else?

Why that happens is the subject of this book.

Much of the evidence supporting the 80% dropout rate is anecdotal. Like an old-fashioned remedy, teenage dropout in swimming is simply a "commonly accepted fact." But that does not mean the dropout rate is any less real. There is good evidence to support this "old wives' tale"—some of it statistical and some anecdotal.

Even something as seemingly trivial as the readership of the swimming blog Jane and I write for is illuminating. *Swimwatch* has been online since 2003 and in its current form since 2009. By March 2017 it had published about 550 stories and had been read by 450,000 readers. Articles have discussed swimming training, administration and international competition. But by far the two most searched and most read stories were written by Jane Copland Pavlovich. Both stories discussed how best to manage the difficulties associated with retiring from swimming. They have been read about 47,000 times; 10.5% of all readers. The subject of when and how to retire clearly causes anxiety. And the concern is reasonable. Self-doubt gnaws at the soul as swimmers ask themselves, "Have I gone as far as I can go; should I go on for one more season; am I being a quitter?" The decision to retire is important. It can positively or negatively colour a swimmer's perception of self.

Some data from New Zealand further illustrates swimming's dropout rate. I prepared a list of the winners of every event in the 2007 and 2010 National Junior Championships. Junior championships in New Zealand are for 10-, 11- and 12-year-old swimmers. This means that the 2010 swimmers in 2017 were 17, 18 and 19, and the 2007 swimmers in 2017 were 20, 21 and 22. So there were two questions: how many of the junior national champions from 2007 and 2010 were still swimming in their late teens and early twenties, and how many were swimming at the same championship winning level?

The answer is that the events at these two junior championships were won by 71 swimmers. Of the 71 swimmers, 58 (82%) were no longer swimming, and 13 swimmers (18%) were still competing. Of those still competing, 5 swimmers (7%) had won a senior national title. So the figures fully support the rule of thumb, 80% dropout rate. However, remember the swimmers studied were the winners, the national junior champions. One would expect their dropout rate to be less. After all, they had tasted success. They had every reason to chase senior international honours. Yet, even in this group the dropout rate was 82%. It could be even higher for less successful swimmers.

At the most recent 2017 New Zealand Age Group Championships, one of the national coaches is reported to have said, "It has been an outstanding week of results for our young swimmers coming up. There have been some really good swims. We have some great kids at all levels and in all strokes coming through. The development of the sport is looking very good in New Zealand."

A few weeks later the national Federation's newsletter reported on the performance of a New Zealand junior team in Australia: "New Zealand's rising swim stars proved the rising quality and depth of the sport in this country with two further records on the final day of the Australian Age Championships in Brisbane."

Swimming federations and national coaches have been saying that sort of thing about their junior swimmers for decades. It has become a cliché. The Saudi Arabian Federation took the "promising juniors" line so far that I was told to forget about the country's senior swimmers and focus on the juniors about to stun the swimming world. Of course, they all ignore the fact that 80% of the "great kids at all levels" are going to be nowhere near a swimming pool in six years. That is an inconvenient truth that needs serious attention.

I expected my analysis of the New Zealand Junior Championship winners to confirm the sport's dropout rate. But two things I did not expect. With the exception of Corey Main and Paige Schendelaar-Kemp, none of the big multiple winners are still swimming. And second, there were a couple of winners who were huge margins ahead of the competition. Katie Hohaia won her 100-meter breaststroke by six seconds. In 2010 she must have been the toast of national swimming. I can imagine she was the first name on the national coach's list of "great kids," but her success was not enough. She joined the 80%.

Dr. John Mullen, editor of the *Swimming Science Research Review*, conducted a study similar to my New Zealand analysis. His findings are published on the website, *Swimming Science*. Mullen looked at swimmers at a much higher level than those in my New Zealand analysis. His study examined 87 swimmers who had competed in the 2008 Junior World Championships and evaluated their performance in the 2012 Olympic Games. Of the 87 swimmers, 66 swimmers (76%) did not participate in the Olympic Games. Of the 21 swimmers (24%) who did qualify to compete in the Games, no one won a medal, and only 3 (4%) managed to qualify for a final.

The following table summarises and compares my New Zealand Junior Championship study results with Dr. Mullen's Junior World Championship results.

ITEM	NZ STUDY		OLYMPIC STUDY	
	NUMBER	%	NUMBER	%
Number of swimmers in study	71	100	87	100
Number of dropouts	58	82	66	76
Number in senior event	13	18	21	24
Number swimming successfully in senior event	5	7	3	4

The studies looked at very different levels of competition—one local and the other international. The findings, however, are remarkably similar. The data confirms that in both studies about three-quarters of the swimmers retire from swimming after their success at a junior event. About one-quarter make it through to the senior ranks, and about 5% are successful. Dropout, it seems, is a problem at all levels of junior swimming. The shift from the junior to the national swimming team is one of the most challenging milestones in a swimmer's career.

My Comet Club team in 1964. I'm second from the right beside my mate, NZ Age Group Champion, Greg Meade. Greg became a swimming coach and for years successfully coached the Comet Club.

CHAPTER 2

IS THERE AN INDIVIDUAL PROBLEM?

Swimmer dropout comes with symptoms. It is important to identify them quickly. The danger is that the symptoms of early dropout only appear when the problem is close to terminal. Left unaddressed, and it is 99% certain to be too late. Teenage dropout can be prevented, but it can seldom be cured. And if remedial steps are not taken quickly, there is no cure.

I want to discuss two cases of swimmers who dropped out before realizing their potential and one case where the swimmer is still competing but will almost certainly have left the sport in the next two years. The three examples demonstrate the performance factors that suggest problems ahead.

The first is a boy who swam for my club in Wellington, New Zealand. We will call him John. He was an amazing talent; good at swimming, athletics and gymnastics. His mother was the driving force behind her son's sport. She was forever coming to my office, usually in an effort to persuade me to increase John's training. Being as the boy was only 12 years old, I, as politely as possible, advised caution. But I knew John was a lost cause when I went to a junior track meet in Wellington one Saturday morning, and there was John, running the 800 meters, long jumping and trying his hand at shot put. That afternoon, I went to watch the annual Vosseler Shield cross-country race. It is a tough and hilly run, climbing and descending 400 feet along the side of Mount Victoria. But John was there, winning the boy's 12 and under event. That evening, I went to the Wellington Regional Aquatic Centre to watch our club swimmers compete in a Wellington league competition. John was there, swimming the 400 IM and the 100 butterfly.

The following Monday, I asked John's mother to come to my office. As gently as I could, I asked whether she thought that perhaps a track meet, a cross-country race and a swim meet on the same day might be overdoing things a bit. I explained that I had coached a number of international athletes, none of whom would attempt a day as tough as the one John had just done. Was she at all concerned that John might burn out early? John's mother looked stunned. Wasn't I aware that her son had won all his events? His father already had the photos framed and displayed on John's bedroom wall. Besides, John just loved the whole day.

I tried to find a way of saying that there are many things children might like, but a parent's job is to decide what is best, not what is liked the most. Clearly my caution was having no effect. Why was I trying to ruin John's athletic career? Why was I trying to stop him having fun? It had been the best day of his sporting life.

I gave up, and so did John when he was just 15 years old. The last time I saw John, he was with some of his mates, about 19 or 20 years old, smoking a cigarette outside the Wellington Railway Station. I guess he was enjoying that as well. However, New Zealand had lost a sporting talent largely because his parents could not control their addiction to seeing their son compete and win swimming and running races.

Arthur Lydiard is quoted as saying, **"There are champions everywhere. Every street has got them. All we need to do is train them properly."** By "train them properly," Lydiard meant observing the disciplines of a well-balanced aerobic, anaerobic and speed programme. In a young athlete's formative development, Lydiard stressed the importance of building an aerobic base. He accepted that the emphasis on aerobic training would probably mean early results would not be as spectacular as swimmers in sprint-trained teams. However, long-term success meant doing the right thing. It meant accepting that swimmers could be lost when parents saw juniors in other teams swimming faster times. But, Lydiard cautioned, good teams need to accept the loss of some swimmers to sprint-based programmes. If the goal of a good programme is to avoid teenage dropout and prepare swimmers for success at the senior level, some families, ambitious for quick results, will move to clubs where immediate fast results are given priority.

When a swimmer transfers out of a well-balanced programme into a sprint programme, Lydiard predicted the swimmer was three steps away from early dropout. The following table shows the three steps.

NAME OF STAGE	CONTENT OF STAGE
Balanced aerobic	Young swimmer is in a balanced programme that accepts slower racing results and prepares athletes for long-term senior success and avoids teenage dropout.
Exploitation	Swimmer transfers to a sprint-based programme and has immediate and often dramatic success as previous aerobic conditioning is exploited. Rapid progress is made for about two years. At this stage the swimmer and parents are certain their decision to change programmes was correct.
Struggle and dropout	Because nothing is done to continue building an aerobic base, progress begins to slow as the early conditioning becomes insufficient to support faster times. Finally, personal best times are not happening, and the swimmer drops out.

Like many Lydiard predictions, this one proved to be accurate. I don't know how many times I have watched swimmers travel from balanced aerobic, to exploitation, to struggle and dropout. Two swimmers illustrate the point. I have chosen them because of their talent. In my coaching career I have been fortunate enough to coach swimmers with extraordinary talent—Rhi Jeffrey and Toni Jeffs, for example. The two junior swimmers in my example had Jeffrey and Jeffs talent. Sadly, they will never achieve their international status. Instead, these young swimmers became classic examples of the path from promising junior to teenage dropout.

First, a swimmer from Delray Beach in Florida. We will call her Anne. She came to the team at age 10 and swam with me doing a balanced programme through to 13 when her parents, hungry for instant results, took her to a sprint programme. Three years later, she changed clubs again, and two years after that, after just one year of college swimming, she retired. Her mother made no secret of the fact that her goal for Anne's swimming was to secure a good university swimming scholarship. I am sure that for two years after changing to the sprint-based programme, both parents were congratulating themselves on making a great choice. Sadly, they were completely oblivious to the cost of their decision, unaware that the aerobic conditioning established in Anne's early training was being exploited far too soon. Anne's talent was easily capable of seeing her complete a successful university swimming career and much more. Her parent's greed ensured that Anne's talent was never realised.

I find a career like Anne's really upsetting. Here was a swimmer who at 12 was ranked in the top 10 of her age group in the United States. And that is a huge accomplishment. She was capable of swimming well under 0.55 seconds for 100 meters and under 1:57 for 200 meters, and it just did not happen.

The following table shows Anne's best long course times each year for the 100-meter freestyle and the 200-meters freestyle. The 400, 800 and 1500 meters show a similar pattern. Anne was most talented over longer distances; that was most likely where her true potential lay.

Anne's Career for 100-Meter and 200-Meter Freestyle

PHASE	YEAR	AGE	TIME	TIME	DISCUSSION
Balanced aerobic	2006	10	1:33	–	A period of aerobic training and steady but not spectacular improvement. Anne improved by an average of 7% per annum in the 100 and 4% in the 200, both ahead of the goal of 3% per annum.
	2007	11	1:16	2.45	
	2008	12	1:11	2.35	
	2009	13	1:06	2.23	
Exploitation	2010	14	1:03	2.14	Anne changed clubs and quickly dropped to 1:01 and 2:10, both an average of about 5% per annum.
	2011	15	1.01	2.10	
Struggle and dropout	2012	16	1:02	2.12	For three years Anne struggled to improve. Her average improvement in both events was less than 1%. At the end of 2014 she dropped out.
	2013	17	1:00	2.10	
	2014	18	1:00	2.09	

My second example is a swimmer in Auckland, New Zealand. We will call her Mary. She is still swimming. Mary began modest aerobic-type training when she was 9. She swam with me through to 12 and then moved to a sprint-based programme. She made spectacular progress for two years. I know her mother was beside herself with joy. On several occasions, she approached other swimmers in my team, recommending the same change. "Just look at how much Mary has improved," she said, completely unaware of the price her daughter was paying for that improvement. Mary is now 15 years old and is one year into the "Struggle" period. Mary's mother had high ambitions for United States university scholarships and international success. Here is a text message she sent to me before Mary moved to the sprint programme: "Buy me a coffee when it's all over. And get my daughter to America." Mary certainly could have gone to the United States, but the figures suggest this is now unlikely. The symptoms have been left unaddressed for too long. In one more year, it will all be over.

Mary's Career for 50-Meter and 100-Meter Backstroke

PHASE	YEAR	AGE	TIME	TIME	DISCUSSION
Balanced aerobic	2011	9	54	-	A period of aerobic training and steady progress. Mary improved by an average of 7% per annum in the 50-meter backstroke and 4% in the 100, both ahead of the goal of 3% per annum.
	2012	10	44	1:33	
	2013	11	40	1:25	
	2014	12	38	1:22	
Exploitation	2015	13	33	1:12	Mary changed clubs and quickly dropped to 33 and 1:10, both an average of about 7% per annum.
	2016	14	33	1:10	
Struggle and dropout	2017	15	34	1.10	After two years exploiting her aerobic conditioning, Mary's progress has stalled. The most likely conclusion? Dropout is probably one year away.

CHAPTER 3

WHAT IS THE CURE?

Measures to prevent teenage dropout should be in place from the beginning of a swimmer's career. Already we have hinted at some factors such as the attitude of parents and coaches, the type of training and the amount of competition. But the cause of teenage dropout that stands above all others is coaching. Excuses such as an interest in boyfriends or girlfriends, injuries and the pressure of study get used to shift the blame, but usually these excuses avoid the real problem: bad coaching. After all, plenty of young people maintain relationships, recover from injuries and do well at school while swimming successfully.

Let's do this properly: a start full of hope and promise, a pool full of dreams.

A strong bond between a coach and swimmer is essential, but it must never be above critical analysis. Swimmers owe a coach loyalty only for as long as they trust the training programme. If that trust is lost, for whatever reason, they should change. My concern for Anne and Mary is not that they left my team but that the programmes they went to have a history of chasing immediate results. Those programmes are enticing to swimmers and parents but seldom result in long-term success.

Administrators and parents who see a high teenage dropout rate need to question the standard of coaching. Every day coaches must make decisions between the competing goals of short-term results and long-term good. Effective coaches almost always rule in favour of long-term good.

Sadly, there are many aspects of good coaching that coaches can get wrong. Some do not understand the principles that they should apply in their programmes. Others, because of financial pressure or competitive ambition, are prepared to sacrifice what is right for what is expedient. They will do whatever it takes to avoid losing members and income or to gain more points in their district championship. For these coaches the lure of short-term success is worth the cost of teenage dropout. The balance of this book will address several coaching decisions that are critical to avoiding teenage dropout.

CHAPTER 4

BUILD A FOUNDATION

Avoiding teenage dropout and successful participation as a senior athlete are dramatically aided when a swimmer's early training focuses on building a substantial aerobic base.

Studies undertaken by the International Centre for Aquatic Research in the United States confirm that anaerobic and speed training at an early age are not only bad, they are probably pointless as well. Aerobic training is the only viable option. Here is what the International Centre for Aquatic Research report says:

> *"Aerobic development is the first factor to reach full development at about 14 years. Prior to this age the primary energy system is endurance, with the prepubescent swimmer having very little anaerobic capacity. Therefore endurance training should begin early and reach a peak in training emphasis by age 14. This approach avoids training designed to highlight a factor not near full development (i.e., anaerobic characteristics) when no adaptation is possible in that system. Endurance-based training may be the single most important component of training throughout the entire career of the athlete."*

The evidence is conclusive: Aerobic conditioning not only does no harm to young swimmers, it is the only training from which immature athletes are physiologically able to secure any benefit.

I suspect very few coaches or parents will be surprised at that finding. In theory the value and importance of aerobic training is understood and has been widely accepted for at least 70 years. The problem is the gap between what is accepted in theory and what is provided in practice. Swimming coaches around the world still insist on giving young swimmers programmes of harsh and often timed sprint training.

In Saudi Arabia I observed a competitive training programme run by a senior national coach. For five weeks I recorded the amount of time spent delivering the three fitness components that must be present in every training programme. The fitness components are:

Aerobic—this describes exercise done at a level at which oxygen is able to supply the swimmer's energy needs.

Anaerobic—this describes what happens when a swimmer goes faster than oxygen can provide and starts to burn sugar as a source of energy.

Speed—this describes the crucial importance of speed in winning swimming races. As Lydiard said, "If you want to be a successful athlete, you have to consider everything. It's no good just thinking about endurance and not developing fine speed."

So a coach's job is to provide these three types of fitness in the correct proportions. And the correct proportions are pretty well known and followed by 99% of the world's good coaches. Whether the proportions are supplied in monthly periods or weekly or daily periods, the proportions are the same. Around the world good coaches provide a balanced programme. That means the aerobic content should occupy 40% of the time, anaerobic content 20% of the time and speed training 40% of the time.

I use a programme of several weeks to provide a 40/20/40 mix of training. The following table shows the periods I allocate in a six-month season.

NAME OF PERIOD	DESCRIPTION	NO. OF WEEKS
Aerobic build-up	Aerobic conditioning threshold swimming	10
Anaerobic	Hard anaerobic interval conditioning	4
Speed	Race preparation and racing	10

That is the gold standard. Successful coaches provide swimmers with a balanced 40/20/40 programme. Duncan Laing, coach of double Olympic Champion Danyon Loader, used much shorter cycles than my programme. He would set three weeks of aerobic swimming, a week of anaerobic and three weeks of speed swimming. I have known coaches who programme their 40/20/40 balance in days: several days of aerobic, a day of anaerobic and several days of speed and racing. These coaches argue that their shorter periods prevent swimmers from getting bored with long periods of the same training. Athlete preference is certainly a factor to consider when plotting how this ratio is applied. I prefer larger blocks allocated to each type of training. Research suggests the longer periods provide better physiological adaptation to each training input. However, debating the use of months, weeks or days is not important. What matters is that the three types of training are provided in a balanced 40/20/40 mix.

So what was the result of my stopwatch study of the national coach's programme in Saudi Arabia? The following table shows what I found and compares it with the training provided by successful coaches.

TYPE OF TRAINING	PERCENT OF TOTAL BY SUCCESSFUL COACHES	PERCENT OF TOTAL IN SAUDI ARABIA
Aerobic	40%	4%
Anaerobic	20%	38%
Speed	40%	58%

Anyone providing swimming training in a 4/38/58 ratio will never win a big swimming race, ever. Not only won't they win international swimming events, young swimmers, tired and beaten up from years of physical hurt, will move on to something more rewarding and less painful.

Since leaving Saudi Arabia, I have heard the national coach has complained about the unnecessary "long hours" involved in an aerobic programme. I have heard the same thing said in New Zealand and in the United States. It is the common fallback position for coaches trying to defend their sprint-based programmes. I guess it is a choice we all must make between "long hours" that achieve something or short sprints that are a cause of the sport's 80% dropout rate and have resulted in the poor performance of programmes such as the one in Saudi Arabia.

My pool in Saudi Arabia, a copy of the Munich Olympic Pool—one of three identical pools built in the Kingdom. Only Saudi Arabia buys Olympic Pools in bulk. The German manufacturer delivered a quality product. The facilities are fully equipped with three pools, saunas, score boards, ice baths, gyms, kitchens, offices, meeting rooms and press facilities. Each pool even has 60 quality stainless steel flag poles—frequently more flag poles than swimmers using the pools

In order to further understand the purpose of build-up aerobic training, I included an analogy in my first book, *"Swim to the Top."* This is what it said:

> *"Companies involved in the forestry industry can operate in one of two ways. They can cut down trees to be used in their mills without replanting the forests behind them. While they are cutting, the mills work well and profits are high. Eventually the trees are all cut, the resources have been used and the mills close. A prudent company however plants one and a half hectares of new trees for every hectare cut. When the first company is closing the other has more resources than when it started. Short-term profits have been reduced by the cost of replanting but without it there is no long-term business. Swimming is the same. The aerobic build-up is the swimmer's time of replanting. It is the period in which athletes increase their resources—resources that are equally beneficial whether the swimmer competes over 50m, 200m or 1500m."*

Like the forestry analogy, the benefits of a build-up are not immediate. Build-up conditioning will not achieve fine results quickly. In fact, progress is normally quite slow. It is, however, the best way to achieve the best results. Over five or six seasons, an aerobically well-conditioned athlete will achieve results their "clear-felled" competition will not be able to match. But more important, an aerobically well-conditioned athlete has not been physically beaten up. Time and fitness have been invested in the athlete rather than taken out. The factors likely to cause early teenage dropout diminish tenfold.

The 40/20/40 balanced programme is based on the experience and results of coaches such as Arthur Lydiard and Cecil Colwin and supported by scientists such as Dr. Peter Snell and the International Centre for Aquatic Research.

In 2009 in *"Runner's World"* Dr. Peter Snell described the importance of aerobic conditioning. Snell was a Lydiard-coached athlete and won three Olympic Gold medals. He now works in the United States and is a world authority on the physical effects of exercise.

"The core of Lydiard training is the quantity and quality of the base training. Long, moderate-pace running is anabolic whereas high-intensity demanding training, while having its place, is catabolic. Thus the base is critical to prevention of overtraining.

Marathon training for an 800m runner is difficult for many coaches and particularly scientists to understand. Many have been quite dismissive about the benefits. To them it makes no sense training slowly for a speed event. The rule of specificity is violated. Why then does it work? Today our knowledge of physiology provides some answers:

- *Long endurance runs appear to provide protection against overtraining from too much high-intensity speed work. Therefore more race-related training may be accomplished.*
- *Activation of fast-twitch muscle fibers is normally accomplished by high-intensity interval runs. We now know that long moderate-pace runs also activate fast-twitch muscle fibers, after slow-twitch fibers have become glycogen depleted after the first one to two hours.*

In sum, and in light of current physiology, there is little I would do differently today. The training of current top athletes is testimony to the relevance of Lydiard training today."

The International Centre for Aquatic Research supports the distinction made between aerobic and anaerobic training inputs. This is what they have to say: "The energy systems (aerobic and anaerobic) adapt independently" and at different rates to "each other to specific modes of training. This is supported by the changes observed in the biochemical markers, PFK and CS. Each of these enzymes changed only in response to specific training: PFK to sprint training, CS to endurance training."

Cecil Colwin in his book, *"Swimming Into the 21st Century,"* wrote, "The development of improved aerobic capacity is a long, slow process requiring a carefully devised long-term plan; by the same token the resulting adaptations will be retained for a long time." About anaerobic training he says, "When it is done properly astonishing improvements can be observed in just six weeks. Its effects are short lived and at times appear volatile. The high-performance level resulting from this training rarely persist more than three months."

The evidence is clear. Good aerobic conditioning as part of a balanced training programme is important in reducing teenage dropout and is the norm at the top levels of the sport. A contributor called Steve, in the running blog "Physi-Kult Running", wrote a brilliant article summarizing the position and importance of aerobic training for young athletes. Although Steve was writing about running, the principles are just as valid in swimming. In fact, given that swimming usually takes place between walls a known distance apart, in lanes only two meters wide and with a coach constantly nearby, Steve's comments are probably more relevant to swimming than running.

> *"In the end, we have to be persistent in pointing out to doubters and the uninformed that high aerobic volume training is the global norm at the top levels of the sport. And, we have to introduce young athletes to this reality from the beginning, even as we scale their programmes to their age and level of experience. The actual amount of easy running that young athletes do is secondary to the general message that simply getting out the door every day to run at an easy pace is the basis of training for this sport. It's what distance runners do the vast majority of the time, and it's what young runners need to become accustomed to if they want to reach their full potential, whatever that may be. We need to teach young runners (and their parents) that it is this, and not so much what happens twice a week at "track practice", that is the principle basis of training to be a runner. The vast majority of young runners will not go on to become serious runners, of course, but this is no excuse for not giving every runner the best chance of maximizing her inherent potential, should she so choose. After all, while we may know that, statistically, most runners who try the sport will not pursue it beyond school age, we do not know who among them just might! There is thus no excuse for foreclosing the options of young runners by taking the line of least resistance in the development of their training programmes."*

To the extent that swim coaches respect these principles the rate of teenage dropout will reduce and the success rate of senior competitors will improve.

The following table sets out the minimum distance of aerobic conditioning I would recommend for swimmers during the build-up portion of their preparation. The importance of aerobic swimming is sufficiently high that national federations should make achieving these distances in swimmer's aerobic training periods a mandatory condition of being selected for open and age group national teams. What seatbelts are to car safety these aerobic distances are to the safety of young swimmers—to reducing swimming's 80% rate of teenage dropout.

AGE (GIRLS)	AGE (BOYS)	AEROBIC MINIMUM WEEKLY DISTANCE (KM)
9 and under	10 and under	No standard
10	11-12	10
11	13	15
12	14	20
13	15	30
14	16	40
15	17	40
16	18	60
17	19	60
18	20	70

Rhi Jeffery: Athen's Olympic Gold medallist, USA National Champion and now head coach of the Cannonball Swim Club in Portsmouth, NH, USA.
© Rhi Jeffrey

Eyad Masoud: Saudi Arabian National Champion, New Zealand National finalist and coach of the Stingrays Swim Team based at the British International School in Jeddah, Saudi Arabia

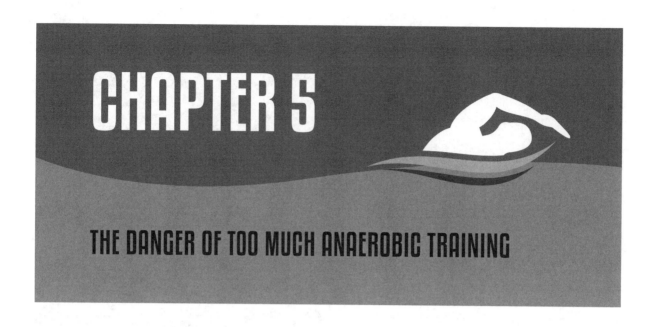

CHAPTER 5

THE DANGER OF TOO MUCH ANAEROBIC TRAINING

The flip side of the value of aerobic conditioning is the danger of excessive anaerobic swimming. We have discussed the futility of anaerobic exercise in immature swimmers. Their capacity to benefit from high-intensity training is limited by their physical immaturity.

But why is anaerobic training dangerous? How much is too much? Why should it be avoided in young swimmers? What harm does it do?

There are practical and academic answers to these questions. One of the best practical examples of the dangers of anaerobic training occurred when I was preparing Toni Jeffs for the Barcelona Olympic Games. Toni had just won a bronze medal in the World Cup Short Course Finals, an event which later became the World Short Course Championships. There was every reason to be confident that she would do well in the Olympic Games. A final was expected, and a medal was possible.

I was convinced that there was no need to do any more aerobic training. The Olympic Games was just a few months away. It was now time to overdose on anaerobic training. When I look back at my training diaries, I cringe in shame. Nothing was good enough. Nothing was fast enough. No set was big enough. One night just before we left for Barcelona, Toni was training in the Wellington Freyberg Pool. I set her a schedule of 20x66 meters. Through the set I pushed and demanded more speed. In the end she swam all 20 in under 40 seconds and still I said it wasn't fast enough. And I was wrong. I believe that set was the straw that broke the camel's back, that guaranteed Olympic disappointment.

It is remarkable that Toni did every meter of what was asked, but she did not survive. By the time we got to Barcelona she was sick and rundown. Eating dinner in a waterfront restaurant two days before her 50 meters freestyle she passed out and slid off her chair unconscious on the ground. Two days later she swam 26.90 to place 27th in the 50-meter freestyle and 58.80 to place 29th in the 100 meters. From 3rd in the world to 27th. From a personal best of 25.54 to 26.90. In the circumstances and given the mistake of far too much speed training, Toni's 26.90 seconds was a stunning effort. And that's how damaging too much anaerobic training can be.

The result hurt, because I knew it was my fault. But the result hurts the athlete far more. It is their result. The victories and the losses belong to the athlete. And for that they deserve our respect and our assurance that we will refrain from invading their joy or their sorrow.

I have never made that mistake again. It is shameful that it took something as big as an Olympic Games blunder to alert me to the dangers of speed. It is off the subject of anaerobic training, but failure does not have many friends.

A week after the Olympic Games, Toni and I were in a nearly empty Koro Lounge at Auckland Airport, waiting for a flight to Wellington. A family group was sitting not far away. The husband walked across to our table and asked, "Are you David Wright and Toni Jeffs?"

I said, "Yes, hello."

He said, "Well I just want you to know that our family got up at one o'clock in the morning to watch you swim, and you let us down."

There was nothing I could say to diminish the swimmer's hurt. What he said was not fair. It was not right. It was ignorant of the facts and oblivious to the pain.

Toni Jeffs swimming at the 1994 Commonwealth Games. Toni had a stroke that everyone admired. In the 1992 World Cup Finals in Majorca the East German National Coach asked if he could film Toni swimming. He wanted to take the film back to Germany and use it as an example of the way swimming should be done. Toni won a bronze medal in the championship.

Academic debate has tended to match those who support aerobic training against those who support anaerobic training. An endless stream of articles endorses the benefits of aerobic conditioning and an equally impressive number of essays promotes the cause of anaerobic training – or, as it is known by the in-crowd, High-Intensity Interval Training. But the debate is pointless. Good swimming demands both types of training. No swimmer is going to be successful by constantly swimming long aerobic sets. Winning swimming races and performing at maximum potential requires the development of speed. And speed requires the input of anaerobic and speed training.

But with equal certainty programmes that overemphasize anaerobic and speed training are not going to yield optimum results. One of the better scientific studies to look at the effect of excessive anaerobic training was undertaken by Laurel MacKinnon at the University of Queensland, Australia. The October 2000 study titled *"Overtraining effects on immunity and performance in athletes"* is reported on the website *Immunology and Cell Biology*.

MacKinnon's study found that a prolonged period of intense anaerobic exercise, something she called overtraining syndrome, is likely to result in poor performance, decreased maximum heart rate, persistent fatigue, illness, poor sleep patterns and fluctuating moods. Other terms used to describe overtraining syndrome include "burnout" and "staleness". These terms describe an athlete's inability to adapt to the cumulative fatigue of frequent intense speed training, not balanced with sufficient rest. Overtraining syndrome, MacKinnon says, is similar in its effect to chronic fatigue and clinical depression. It is serious.

In addition, several immune factors may be curbed by prolonged periods of intense anaerobic training. These include altered blood lactate concentration during severe exercise, signs of respiratory infection, damage to white blood cells and reduced blood antibodies affecting the control of infections in body tissue including the capacity to repair the damage resulting from training stress.

MacKinnon noted that the intense, anaerobic nature of many swimming programmes makes swimmers particularly vulnerable to overtraining syndrome. Anaerobic threshold is a good indicator of each swimmer's capacity to perform endurance exercise. The onset of fatigue, as measured by their anaerobic threshold, occurs 20 to 30% sooner in overtrained swimmers. Their ability to sustain intense training and their competitive performance are weakened.

Studies in a variety of sports suggest that overtraining can reduce competitive performance by as much as 20%. In swimming the margin between winning and losing is always a lot less than that. For example, FINA qualifying times required to compete in the Olympic Games are normally only 4 to 5% slower than the world record. In the Rio Olympic Games, the average gap between first and last in the finals was 2.6%.

In the case of Toni Jeffs being overtrained prior to the Barcelona Olympic Games, recovery was a long process. It took months for Toni to return to her best form. This is not unusual. Recovery normally requires two or three weeks of complete rest followed by a period of eight weeks of easy swimming. When this sort of recovery is necessary for a world class swimmer, it is not hard to imagine how destructive overtraining can be for junior swimmers.

Whole careers can be put at risk. Even though Toni qualified for the next New Zealand team selected after the Barcelona Olympic Games, she was not selected. I did hear that her poor performance at the Olympics may have been the cause. In these circumstances career-altering events such as a loss of sponsorship income can follow. In junior swimmers the problems associated with overtraining are less complex but are just as severe. Junior swimmers simply reason that they are not good enough, not tough enough to hack the work involved and retire from the sport – another addition to the 80%.

Swimming is particularly vulnerable to overtraining. Weight-bearing and contact sports have some protection because overuse incurs the more obvious risks of muscle, tendon and bone injury. Overtraining syndrome in swimming is less obvious than these injuries, but its consequences are just as serious. Laurel MacKinnon estimates that at any one time between 7 and 20% of all athletes demonstrate signs of overtraining. It is expected that swimming, because participants train throughout the year, six or seven days a week and for four to six hours a day, will have incidents towards the higher end of that scale.

And yet in spite of all the evidence, in spite of all the study, it is amazing the number of programmes that still make my Barcelona mistakes: too much anaerobic training, inadequate aerobic conditioning, not enough rest and wasted speed work in young children. These are bad errors. They cause hurt and harm.

Eyad Masoud in Jeddah, Saudi Arabi, swimming his May 2017 aerobic build-up; 60 kilometers in one week is not easy.

CHAPTER 6

WHAT DOES ANAEROBIC TRAINING LOOK LIKE?

Many coaches lack an understanding of the difference between aerobic, anaerobic and speed training. I have already mentioned the coaches who have said to me that they follow the Lydiard principle of establishing an aerobic foundation before setting sessions of hard anaerobic training. Yet their programmes are nothing like the aerobic, anaerobic and speed schedules characteristic of a balanced Lydiard programme.

For example, Coach Kimberly was a good assistant coach who worked for me in Auckland. I arranged for her to take part in a Swimming New Zealand coaching accreditation course. The weekend programme included watching the Swimming New Zealand national team coaches take a training session. When the course ended, I was interested to hear what Kimberly had seen and learned.

She mentioned that she was surprised at the difference between the "aerobic" training used in our programme and the "aerobic" training given to the national team. I asked if she had an example of an aerobic schedule used on her course, and could I see it? Here is what was written on the New Zealand National Training Centre's white board; this is what a senior performance coach gave to his swimmers as an aerobic training schedule.

DISTANCE	METHOD
Warm-up	**Aerobic and skills**
4x150	50 free and 50 fists and 50 free – take one less stroke each 150
2x100	Kick in four positions
2x150	Back 6 underwater kicks off the walls, good streamlines and breakouts
2x100	Kick in four positions
2x150	Pull buoy, 100 moderate and 50 breathes every 5 strokes hard
8x25	Fins, odd underwater 15 fast, even dead start flags to flags sprint
Main set – aerobic	**Heart rate 50 beats below maximum**
1x200	On 3.00 then 4x50 #1 drill main stroke
2x200	On 2.55 then 4x50 "King Fish" tumble main stroke
3x200	On 2.50 then 4x50 free jump outs
4x200	On 2.45 then 4x50 sprint middle 20 meters as a "King Fish" tumble
	Dives and skills

The reason for Coach Kimberly's confusion is apparent. Customary aerobic conditioning is based on the teachings of master track coaches, Arthur Lydiard and Arch Jelley. I began my coaching career in a sport where aerobic conditioning meant spending two hours running at a firm pace through the Waitakere Ranges in Auckland or along forest trails in Boulder, Colorado, or down a dusty road in Kenya's Rift Valley. What does the New Zealand national coach's fruit salad mix of interval repetitions have to do with that sort of international aerobic training? The answer is, of course, nothing.

Certainly, aerobic means the same thing in the world of swimming as it does in running. The problems highlighted by the national coach's programme are not unique to the National Training Centre. Many swimming coaches suffer from the problem of not understanding the nature, effect and importance of genuine aerobic training. While Wikipedia may not be the soundest source of coaching information, its definition of aerobic exercise is pretty accurate:

"Aerobic exercise is physical exercise of relatively low intensity and long duration, which depends primarily on the aerobic energy system. Aerobic means 'with oxygen', and refers to the use of oxygen in the body's metabolic or energy-generating process. Many types of exercise are aerobic, and by definition are performed at moderate levels of intensity for extended periods of time."

As you can see, the emphasis is on low or moderate levels of intensity for long or extended periods of time. There is none of that in the programme presented to New Zealand's best swimmers. In fact, the programme is full of expressions relevant to tough anaerobic workouts.

For example: "Breathe every five strokes **hard**". The word aerobic means with oxygen, which makes it difficult to understand why this coach limits breathing to every five strokes and still calls the swims aerobic. That sort of breath control is a defining characteristic of anaerobic training, not aerobic. And, of course, the word "hard" is even underlined in case we hadn't got the point that this coach thinks that 2x150 done hard fits comfortably into an aerobic training schedule.

"8x25 underwater 15 meters fast". The word "fast" does not appear in Wikipedia's definition either. Come to think of it, in 10 years of listening to Lydiard and Jelley discuss the importance of aerobic training, I never heard them use the word "fast".

"Dead start, flags to flags sprint". Now here is something new—aerobic sprints; the attraction of opposites.

"4x50 jump outs". This exercise involves sprinting 25 meters, climbing out to run around the starting block and sprinting 25 meters back down the pool. Even the most generous supporter of high-performance coaching might find that stretching the definition of "low intensity for a long duration". It will be valuable, though, when sprinting around the starting blocks becomes an Olympic event. In the meantime, it has no place in a programme called "aerobic and skills".

"Sprint middle 20 meters as a 'King Fish' tumble". A "King Fish" turn involves diving under the water at the flags, turning at the wall still under the water and swimming to the flags again before coming back to the surface. I'm not sure why anyone would include an exercise clearly designed to deprive the swimmer of oxygen in a programme that twice has the label of "aerobic".

Even the idea of descending a set of 200s is hard to characterize as truly aerobic.

The good news is that the programme includes a definition of what the coach means by aerobic swimming. It says swimmers should hold a heart rate of 50 beats below their maximum. That is a pretty good guide. A swimmer with a maximum heart rate of 210 beats per minute should stay under 160. What is impossible, of course, is to "sprint" the "hard", "fast", "King Fish", "jump out" intervals in this programme and still have a heart rate under a 160 beats a minute. The author defines the word "aerobic" and then sets a swimming programme incapable of being swum in accordance with the definition. I asked Olympic gold medallist, Rhi Jeffrey, if this programme met her understanding of an aerobic schedule. I thought she was going to die laughing as she answered, "Of course not."

The really sad aspect of this example is the programme was used during a seminar to tutor young coaches. Ten trainee coaches left this seminar believing that 8x25 meter sprints is a recommended example of aerobic conditioning. Anyone attending a training course has a right to expect better than this nonsense. The trainee coaches are going to return to their home programmes where they will coach pre-teen and teenage swimmers. No one should be surprised when the young swimmers in their clubs begin to drop out of the sport. Their coaches have been taught that sound aerobic conditioning includes a daily grind of high-intensity interval training.

I know another New Zealand coach who regularly puts up training sessions that include big interval sets that he calls aerobic to be done at a heart rate of no less than 10 beats below maximum. Given that his swimmers probably have maximum heart rates around 210 bpm, he is saying his swimmers should train for 40 minutes or so holding a heart rate of more than 200 bpm. Apart from the fact that it is probably impossible to do, the damage done to the junior swimmers who try will be terminal.

The same coach trained a very good backstroke swimmer. At a regional championship I noticed she was not swimming well. Her skin was in terrible condition, and I heard she had been affected by several bad colds. The problem was overtraining; the cure was rest. At training the following week, I was not surprised to see the swimmer working through a set of 60x25 meter sprints. Her coach had no idea of the damage he was

Swim teacher's course graduation in Jeddah, Saudi Arabia. This group was drilled on the difference between aerobic, anaerobic and speed. (I am on the far left.)

doing. All he understood was, she swam slowly; she must need more training. The swimmer lasted a few more months before retiring from swimming. If you observe symptoms of overtraining and do nothing or increase the training intensity and volume, the problems will get increasingly severe. Eventually the athlete will need a very long break to recover or, as is often the case, will give the whole sport away as a waste of time.

We have discussed what aerobic swimming is not, but we need to also look at what aerobic swimming is. Written on a white board, aerobic sets can look very similar to high-performance interval training. The difference is often not in the programme but in the way the programme is swum. For example, 15x100 can be aerobic or anaerobic. Each 100-meter swum hard with three minutes rest makes 15x100 an anaerobic set. During a set like that, the swimmer's heart rate is likely to climb over 200 bpm – well into the anaerobic range. Done at a modest pace on a 1.30 interval and the same set is aerobic. The heart rate of a competent swimmer in a set swum at this speed will be 150 bpm to 160 bpm, well inside the limit for aerobic swimming.

Distance helps limit the danger of excessive anaerobic stress. During the aerobic conditioning period I make selective use of longer swims of between 2,000 and 10,000 metres. At a club training camp, I did see one of New Zealand's best distance swimmers, Phillipa Langrell, complete an 8,000-meter medley swim. Since then I have also set 4,000- and 8,000-metre medley swims. For several years my best swimmers, including national representatives Rhi Jeffrey, Jane Copland Pavlovich, Toni Jeffs and Nichola Chellingworth, swam 100x100 meters on 1.30 every Saturday morning. This was my equivalent of Lydiard's 24-mile tough Waitakere Ranges run.

Clearly the temptation to go excessively anaerobic is reduced when the swim is an 8,000 medley or 100x100. That is not to say long swims avoid anaerobic mechanisms. Swum fast enough, even long swims will have an anaerobic content. The important point is to emphasize the reason for swimming the set. Whether the training programme is aerobic, anaerobic or speed, it is essential swimmers understand the purpose of the training and how it should be swum. This, of course, is especially true with young swimmers who are learning how the training is intended to affect them physiologically. That knowledge means they are better prepared for the training, they will do the training better, and they will achieve better results.

Without this understanding there is a real danger that swimmers, especially young swimmers, will want to swim everything as fast as possible. Their logic is – the faster I train, the better I will be. That is a message that often gets reinforced by coaches and at home. But swimmers cannot obtain optimum results that way.

Even some school PE teachers who have spent four years at university earning a degree in physical education appear to have little understanding of the difference between aerobic and anaerobic. About a week after Jane won the New Zealand open short course 200 meters breaststroke title, her school report was delivered. The only subject noting a problem was PE. There in the comments section the teacher had written, "Lacks aerobic fitness". Being as Jane was probably one of the aerobically fittest people in the country at the time, I wondered how the teacher had reached that stunning conclusion. Jane explained that she had been asked to do an anaerobic basketball beep test a few hours after her morning 6-kilometer swim session. It was the wrong test, done at the wrong time and came to the wrong conclusion.

I have often been subject to criticism from those who find fault in long aerobic training. They accuse aerobic programmes of being a cause of the dropout problem. It needs to be understood that extreme sessions, such as the Saturday 100x100 used by the critics to disparage aerobic programmes, are only given to senior experienced swimmers. For example, in my New Zealand team I only had six swimmers on the full programme. Four were open national championship swimmers and one was an Olympic Gold medallist. And this is also not to say that those sessions and an aerobic programme as a whole were not tough; it takes a lot of mental stamina to get through sessions like this week after week. But these sessions and this programme will not result in harmful physical repercussions.

The sixth swimmer completing the weekly 100x100 was Abigail. We have already mentioned her capacity for work. She was one of those characters who thrive and prosper on a diet of distance. In the six-week build-up that included the 100x100s, she swam 85, 85, 101, 90, 90 and 90 kilometers. I would defy anyone to describe this young woman as anything but committed and excited by her journey through swimming. However, even she surprised me one morning. Her training day was planned as 10,000 meters in the morning and 8,000 in the afternoon. The morning session was 3×1000, 10×200, 1×1000 kick, 20×100, 1×1000 kick, 500 swim, 500 kick. That is an aerobic session. The afternoon session was not a lot different. Unfortunately, the afternoon session was in doubt. A meeting meant she would not be able to get to the pool, but there was a solution. Could she, I was asked, swim both the morning and afternoon sessions in the morning? After all it was only 18,000 meters. If she began at 5.30am she would be done by 10.30am.

What would you have done? I have no doubt there are critics expecting all sorts of ruin – broken shoulders and broken spirits. I questioned the sense of it for about two minutes. Then I thought of Lydiard, Quax, Farah and others running up to 200 miles a week in pursuit of their dream. Who was I to deny their swimming likeness? At 10.30am I got a text message. It said, "I did the 18 btw. I think I might come in and do another 8 tonight. Just kidding!"

There is something good about that story: a young woman setting goals, meeting challenges and winning. Whatever her race results might be she knows, I know and her parents know she has set herself training goals of the highest standard and she has prevailed. No one will ever take that away from her. Of course, she should have swum the 18,000.

When I came back to New Zealand after seven years in the United States, I was told to forget all that distance stuff. New Zealand swimmers will never do it, they said. I did not believe that. The spirit of Jelley, Lydiard, Snell, Quax, Dixon and Walker is as alive and well today as it ever was. I have seen today's generation do some remarkable things.

Jane swam 800 meters without stopping when she was three. She did 1,000 kilometers in 10 weeks when she was 16. Toni Jeffs twice reached 1,000 kilometers in 10 weeks. Even Nichola Chellingworth, who was no great lover of distance conditioning, regularly reached 800 kilometers in a 10-week build-up. Every week, during the build-up, Rhi Jeffrey swam in excess of 80 kilometers. National open championship bronze medallist, Jessica Marston, was always around 90 kilometers a week. The American, Joseph Skuba, a 50-second long course 100-meter swimmer, swam over 900 kilometers in all his build-ups. And, of course, Abigail swam 18 kilometers in one training session. None of these swimmers are injured or broken. All of them were or are fine athletes. Yes, there is plenty of evidence to suggest the doubters are wrong. It is reasonable to leave the final view on this subject to Dr. Peter Snell.

United Club member and New Zealand's best swimmer, Lauren Boyle, gives a boost to two of our West Auckland club juniors – the mark of a champion.

AEROBIC CONDITIONING DISCUSSED BY DR. PETER SNELL

Arthur Lydiard based stock in his elaborate schedules. He talked about balancing the training. My conclusion is that the details were relatively unimportant though I didn't realize that until 1962. That was when I did his schedule and trained right through when I ran my World Records when I "wasn't supposed to" based on the schedule. Like Marty Liquori said, all you need is a decent base, some leg turnover work and a lot of the scientific stuff is bullshit. Many American runners run themselves into the ground because that is what the coaches think they need to do. When you have done distance for many months you feel that you have lost your speed so many runners stopped the Lydiard distance and started doing a bunch of speed work and they raced well. Then they concluded that since they saw the light they didn't need the distance work. Then the following season, without the base, they don't race as well. Later on, as a scientist, I learned that the benefits of distance running are achieved after muscle glycogen depletion. So if you run for two hours a lot of the slow-twitch muscle fibres which were initially recruited run out of glycogen and cannot contract any more. Eventually you use the fast twitch muscle fibres which you normally only use when running fast, so that was a stunning revelation for me. I didn't know that when I was running my 22-milers. I just knew that the quality of my build-up work had a great relation to how I raced later on the track.

I tried to run everything evenly, so we didn't do those sessions where a runner gets faster as he progresses. I also didn't do sessions where I went from 200 meters to 400 meters to 600 meters and back down. I think those are little tricks that coaches use to justify their existence. It's all bullshit. As long as you get an endurance base and avoid the pitfalls of overtraining you will improve. The ideal training is the maximum amount of race-related pace running you can do without overtraining. That implies that you must have the base before to allow you to avoid overtraining.

Learn to Swim graduation in Jeddah, Saudi Arabia

But will they be around to join Eyad Masoud as he prepares for morning training in Jeddah, Saudi Arabia?

CHAPTER 7

WHAT SHOULD THE SWIMMER KNOW?

In the previous chapter we stressed the importance of swimmers understanding the theoretical purpose of their training. This chapter will discuss the practical information that should be taught to swimmers. This is the knowledge of training principles swimmers need to understand in order to obtain maximum benefit from their training.

Coaches have two options. Some see their role as writing training on the team white board and then making sure it gets done. Explaining the reason and purpose of the programme is not important. But then really they are not coaches at all. They fail the first test, that of communicating knowledge. Good coaches are educators who recognize that swimmers perform better when they know why they are swimming a set in a certain way. I prefer this approach and enjoy being called a teacher rather than a coach. The word "teacher" fits more comfortably with how I view my role in the swimmer's life.

AEROBIC TRAINING

Aerobic describes training designed to lift the athlete's ability to exercise using oxygen as the primary source of energy. It generally involves steady-state swimming at or below a heart rate of 160 beats per minute. The distances swum during an aerobic training period can be quite high. I have had many swimmers average 100 kilometres a week for a 10-week aerobic training period. One open water swimmer did a 10-week aerobic period of training averaging 120 kilometres a week. At the end of that build-up she was second in the national 5,000 meters open water championship and was selected in the national open water team.

Major improvements in aerobic speed are possible as a result of good, steady-pace conditioning. The following table shows Jane Copland Pavlovich's average training time in her first season of senior training for each distance and her average training time for the same set four years later. It is important to keep in mind this improvement and all these times were achieved at the same aerobic effort – that is, at a heart rate of less than 160 bpm. Over 1,000 metres, for example, swimming "easily" in year one Jane swam each repetition in 13:00. Four years later, at the same effort, each swim was 1minute, 11seconds faster.

The starting point before she began to push for anaerobic speed was so much faster. Clearly a swimmer starting to call on their anaerobic fitness at 11:49 pace is going to race faster than a swimmer who goes anaerobic at 13:00 pace. In fact, many swimmers with a substantial aerobic base can swim faster, below 160 bpm heart rate, than poorly trained swimmers can swim anaerobically. And in this improvement lies the secret of successful coaching and also the secret to reducing the incidence of overtraining syndrome and teenage dropout.

Aerobic Sets Jane Copland Swam in Year One and Year Five

YEAR	DISTANCE OF REPETITION	AVERAGE TIME
1	12x500	6:21.92
5	12x500	5:40.30
1	6x1000	13:00.00
5	6x1000	11:49.00
1	15x400	5:12.00
5	15x400	4:41.65
1	30x200	2:35.80
5	30x200	2:18.77
1	4x1500	20:09.45
5	4x1500	17:54.00
1	2x3000	38:49. 00
5	2x3000	36:57.00

Several physiological changes occur that result in these large improvements in performance. Aerobic conditioning increases capillary density and promotes the growth of new capillaries. Although an increase in the number of capillaries is important, the major effect of aerobic training on capillaries involves improving those that the swimmer already has. Aerobic exercise promotes oxygen exchange by increasing the surface area of both the venous and arterial capillaries. Clearly an athlete with more capillaries providing muscles with more oxygen more efficiently will experience improved performance.

Other physiological changes include a lower heart rate and increased stroke volume of the heart. Lower blood viscosity further improves cardiac output. Research also indicates that the enzymes required to form ATP can increase 2.5 times. And, myoglobin, the oxygen and iron binding compound, has been found to increase by up to 80%.

Recent studies, particularly those by Dr. Peter Snell at the University of Texas, have also established that training at moderate aerobic pace improves fast-twitch fibre racing speed. Swim for long enough, and eventually slow-twitch fibres used to handle that pace will become depleted of their glycogen reserves. The ability of the muscles to contract becomes impaired. The body responds by recruiting fast-twitch fibres to compensate. And so, contrary to the opinion of many critics, long aerobic training does exercise fast-twitch muscle fibre.

What this means is there are two ways to exercise the athlete's fast-twitch fibres. One is by high-intensity interval training, and the other is by doing distance aerobic swimming at a moderate pace. The pace cannot be slow. But then, 36:57 for a female 3,000-metre swimmer is not slow, but for an aerobically well-conditioned swimmer represents a moderate pace.

In summary, the purpose of the aerobic period is to improve the speed at which a swimmer can swim aerobically. This is done by adding capillaries, improving the performance of the existing capillaries, improving heart, lung and blood function, and exercising slow- and fast-twitch muscle fibres.

Jane Copland Pavlovich: New Zealand Champion, record holder and representative at the Oceania Championships and Pan Pacific Games. The big return for Jane from 16,813 kilometers swum in training in New Zealand was earning a four-year scholarship to swim and study at Washington State University. Education scholarships in the USA lift the level of world swimming and are a valuable reward for the hard work always involved in being accepted into a NCAA Division One team.

ANAEROBIC TRAINING

This period of training adds to the aerobic base by training the swimmer to tolerate the discomfort associated with race pace effort. Training becomes anaerobic when the level of intensity exceeds the athlete's capacity to provide the energy required with oxygen. When this occurs, the swimmer uses glucose stored in the muscle cells as a fuel. The result of using glucose is the formation and discomfort of lactic acid. Traditionally the accumulation of lactic acid has been accepted as a primary cause of reduced muscle efficiency. Modern research suggests that serious muscle fatigue is more complex than just the accumulation of lactic acid. What has not changed, however, is the principle that raised muscle and blood lactate concentrations are a normal result of physical effort. The effectiveness of anaerobic activity can be improved through training. Improvements are, however, limited and are achieved quite quickly.

The nature of anaerobic exercise sets a number of characteristics and limits that should apply to this period of training. Less time should be allocated to anaerobic training than aerobic or speed training. A balanced programme means addressing aerobic training 40% of the time, speed training 40% of the time and anaerobic training just 20% of the time. The shorter time allocated to anaerobic training is appropriate because of two qualities that characterize this period. First, anaerobic training is severe – it hurts. And second, training the swimmer's body to tolerate the discomfort associated with the accumulation of lactic acid happens quite quickly. There is no need for longer than four weeks of anaerobic training. The necessary anaerobic adaptations will have occurred in that time.

In order to secure the best anaerobic outcome, training sets are designed to replicate the stress experienced in a race by promoting the build-up of lactic acid in muscles and in the blood stream.

When I first began setting anaerobic sessions, my programmes were too short and too severe. I had Toni Jeffs do sessions like 5x100 on 5.00 minutes. Toni did them well. They were fast, each one under a minute, but she was not getting anaerobically fit. Something was wrong. I asked Lydiard why things were not going as they should. He explained that I was not observing the 30-minute rule required to secure good anaerobic conditioning.

In order to obtain the best anaerobic result, in order for full fatigue to take place, anaerobic exercise has to continue for about 30 minutes. Much shorter than that and the muscles will "lactate out", but the comprehensive alteration of venous and arterial blood will not have had time to occur. Exercise for much longer than 30 minutes will not be severe enough to obtain the best anaerobic result.

In my 5x100 example, Toni was exercising for less than 5 minutes, well short of the 30 minutes required to experience full anaerobic fatigue. So the 30-minute rule achieves the best anaerobic result by being the most severe, by causing the highest level of anaerobic damage. And for this very reason anaerobic training has only a limited place in the preparation of pre-teen and early teen swimmers. Follow the 30-minute rule with young swimmers for several months, and early dropout is a guaranteed result. The hurt is just too great. The damage is just too severe.

Even in older athletes the application of anaerobic training requires caution. Anaerobic conditioning is physiologically very different from aerobic training. Cecil Colwin in his fine book, *"Swimming Into the 21st Century"*, wrote, "The development of improved aerobic capacity is a long, slow process requiring a carefully devised long-term plan; by the same token the resulting adaptations will be retained for a long time." About anaerobic training, however, he writes, "When it is done properly astonishing improvements can be observed in just six weeks. Its effects are short lived and at times appear volatile. The high-performance level resulting from this training rarely persist more than three months."

Taking all these factors into account, I now allocate four weeks every six-month season to specific anaerobic training. In each of the four weeks I prepare three anaerobic 30-minute sets. That's a total of 12 anaerobic sessions every six months, or 24 sessions each year. And that anaerobic work load, remember, is for well-trained senior swimmers. Junior swimmers should never be set more than two anaerobic sessions in a week and only ever for a maximum of four weeks in a six-month season. If in doubt, do less.

The following tables shows the sets used for mature swimmers in the four-week anaerobic period and how the senior programme is modified for junior swimmers.

For a 50 and 100 Swimmer

DAY	WEEKS	MATURE SWIMMERS	JUNIOR SWIMMERS
Monday	1 and 3	6x400	6x300
Wednesday	1 and 3	45x50	–
Saturday	1 and 3	16x150	45x50
Monday	2 and 4	12x200	24x100
Wednesday	2 and 4	32x75	–
Saturday	2 and 4	24x100	32x75

For a 100 and 200 Swimmer

DAY	WEEKS	MATURE SWIMMERS	JUNIOR SWIMMERS
Monday	1 and 3	6x500	6x400
Wednesday	1 and 3	24x100	–
Saturday	1 and 3	8x300	24x100
Monday	2 and 4	6x400	12x200
Wednesday	2 and 4	16x150	–
Saturday	2 and 4	12x200	16x150

For a 200 and 400 Swimmer

DAY	WEEKS	MATURE SWIMMERS	JUNIOR SWIMMERS
Monday	1 and 3	3x1000	3x800
Wednesday	1 and 3	12x200	–
Saturday	1 and 3	6x500	12x200
Monday	2 and 4	4x600	6x400
Wednesday	2 and 4	8x300	–
Saturday	2 and 4	6x400	8x300

It is important to have at least a portion of these anaerobic sets done as kick. Leg muscles need to receive specific anaerobic attention. In the 24x100 set, for example, I usually set 20x100 as swim and 4x100 as kick. The Australian coach, Peter Freney, alerted me to the importance of doing a portion of these sets as kick. He was convinced my swimmers were not finishing as well as they should because their kick was letting them down. He was right. Including a portion of the anaerobic sets as leg training resulted in a marked improvement in their race results.

In my first book, *Swim to the Top*, I named the chapter on anaerobic training *"Festina Lente"*, a Latin expression meaning "make haste slowly". That caution is important to planning good anaerobic training for senior swimmers. It is however critical to completing successful anaerobic training for junior team members.

SPEED TRAINING

This final period of each season's training offers the least danger to young swimmers. It is time to go racing; time to reap the rewards of the training done in the aerobic and anaerobic periods. Because it is time to go fast, the key words describing these 10 weeks are "fresh and sharp". No one should be overtraining at this stage. Lydiard succinctly said, "You can't run around the Waitakere Ranges and a four-minute mile at the same time". Long distances and hard anaerobic sets are a thing of the past. It is now time to race.

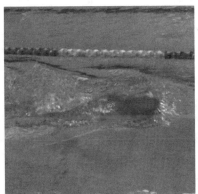

Bounding, chicken wings and Janet Evans are three good sprint drills.

Each week through the 10-week speed training period follows a standard pattern. The first table following shows the format followed by senior, mature swimmers. The second table shows the format followed by junior inexperienced swimmers. Additional sessions over and above those shown in the tables are programmed as aerobic recovery training.

Speed Training for Mature Swimmers

DAY	TYPE OF TRAINING
Monday	Sprints
Tuesday	Fartlek
Wednesday	Time trial
Thursday	Review
Friday	Easy aerobic
Saturday	Time trial
Sunday	Easy aerobic

Speed Training for Junior Swimmers

DAY	TYPE OF TRAINING
Monday	Sprints
Tuesday	Easy aerobic
Wednesday	Time trial
Thursday	Review
Friday	Easy aerobic
Saturday	Fartlek
Sunday	–

Sprints on Monday get the week off to a fast start. They remind the swimmer that the time has come to swim fast. Gennadi Touretski, coach of Alexander Popov, accurately said, "Speed is the most precious thing. It is what we are about. It is what we are trying to achieve." The weeks of aerobic conditioning and tough anaerobic swimming will have temporarily blunted a swimmer's racing speed. The time has come to get that back. There are numerous sprint programmes that can be used in this Monday session. The following table shows some sets I use to sharpen a swimmer's speed.

SESSION NAME	SESSION DESCRIPTION
Sprints	Sets done as 15-, 25- or 50-meter sprints with good recovery. Normally do between 10 and 20 repetitions. Also include kick.
In/Out	Sets done as 5-, 8- or 10-meter swims into the wall and turn to sprint same distance back out.
Out/In	Same as above but done sprinting away from the wall with turn in the middle of the pool and return to the wall.
5/11/3/7	Dive, sprint out for five strokes, turn in mid-pool, back in eleven strokes, turn, out in five strokes, turn in mid-pool again and back to finish at wall in seven strokes. All sprinting. All good underwater kicks.
H2O kick	Kick 5 seconds against wall, flip, fly kick 15 meters under water and three fast strokes.
11 strokes	From a dive or push off, sprint 11 strokes at 50, 100, 200 or 400 racing turnover and size. Time 10 strokes to determine race rhythm.
Sprint with fins	Sets done as 15-, 25- or 50-meter sprints with good recovery but with fins to exaggerate sensation of speed. Do between 5 and 10 repetitions.
Long bungy	Sprint 25 meters being towed to faster speed by long bungy cord.
Building swims	Swim 25 or 50 meters starting very slow with big DPS and building rhythm until arms are going faster than race speed in last five meters.
Fast arms crazy	Swim 11 strokes away from wall with maximum arm speed – far faster than in a race.

On Tuesday, I programme a fartlek session. Fartlek is a term used first by Swedish runners meaning "speed play". In running, fartlek training involves easy running for a distance, sprinting for a short distance, back to easy running, up to medium speed running, followed by another sprint and some more easy running – all done in an unstructured way. In swimming it is difficult to mimic the unstructured nature of fartlek running. Instead, I set a distance between 400 and 1500 meters made up of either 12.5 fast/12.5 easy or 25 fast/25 easy or 50 fast/50 easy or 50 fast/25 easy. During the session, I nominate whether the fast swims should be swum at 50, 100, 200 or 400 race pace. Frequent alterations of pace, even within the same fartlek set, are good for teaching and consolidating the pace required for each competition distance.

I allocate one day each week to fartlek swimming because it is such a very good transition exercise. It quickly restores swimmers' speed. The alternating effort seems to stimulate swimmers mentally and physically to the demands of fast swimming. As a result, fartlek adds speed quicker than many other forms of speed training.

Time trials or races are included on Wednesday and Saturday each week. These are critical to the success of the speed training period. In these 10 weeks, the aim is to swim a total of around 50 races prior to the season's pinnacle event at the end of week 10. With heats and finals, six or seven meets of four events each will quickly reach the 50-race total. For junior swimmers, especially, do not race more than 50 races in a season. No matter how much they appear to enjoy racing, stick to the 50 races per season rule. Racing is demanding and usually involves physical hurt. Its cumulative hurt can cause permanent damage and early retirement. 50 race efforts in a season, 100 in a year are plenty for anyone.

In order to swim well in the end of season main event, a swimmer needs three qualities: the speed required, the endurance necessary and the correct race plan. The time trial and race sessions on Wednesday and

Saturday provide the opportunity to put in place these three qualities. In the 10 weeks swimmers are going to swim a time trial or race twice every week. I select trials and races that are shorter than, longer than and the same as the distance of the season's main event. Shorter trials are used to test speed, longer trials to test endurance and same distance trials to test the swimmer's race plan.

For example, a specialist 100-meter swimmer would use 25-, 50- and 75-meter trials to test speed and 125, 150 and 200 trials to test endurance. Trials over 100 meters would test the swimmer's race plan.

From a young age, swimmers should be taught the importance of pace, stroke counts and stroke rhythm. All three are critical skills required to execute a well-planned race. All three need frequent practice. As swimmers mature they need to be able to swim any predetermined distance at a known pace, in a known stroke rhythm, at a known stroke count. For example, a good female freestyle swimmer might be asked to swim 25 meters in 12.5 seconds, in 19 strokes and at a stroke rate of 0.75 seconds per stroke. Whatever race formula is set, the swimmer should hit the formula every time without error. I practice this skill frequently in the speed period by changing the pace, the rhythm and the stroke count required during the Monday sprint sessions and the two time trial sessions. Pace, rhythm and stroke count are basic tools of the swimmer's trade.

The optimum pace, rhythm and stroke count formula will vary, of course, depending on a swimmer's sex, their age, their ability and the race distance. Determining the ideal formula requires constant testing and practice. As swimmers mature and their speed improves the best number of strokes and the rhythm formula will also change and require practice to fix in place, ready to be used in a race.

So, as swimmers gain experience, improving their performance changes from "dive in, swim fast and hope" to "how well can I execute a pre-determined race plan of pace, stroke counts and rhythm"?

The following table shows a short course 200-meter breaststroke race plan prepared for Jane Copland Pavlovich. The aim was to break the open New Zealand record.

Jane's 200-meter Breaststroke Race Plan October 2001

LAP	START DISTANCE	START TIME	SWIM DISTANCE	SWIM TIME	STROKES	TOTAL TIME	50S TIME
1	10.00	6.00	15.00	10.50	8	16.50	
2	7.00	6.20	18.00	12.80	9	19.00	35.50
3	7.00	6.20	18.00	12.80	9	19.00	
4	7.00	6.20	18.00	12.80	9	19.00	38.00
5	7.00	6.20	18.00	12.80	9	19.00	
6	7.00	6.20	18.00	12.90	9	19.10	38.10
7	7.00	6.30	18.00	12.90	9	19.20	
8	7.00	6.30	18.00	12.90	9	19.20	38.40
TOTAL						150.00	150.00
						2:30.00	

In the speed period of training, Jane practiced this plan in each week's time trial sessions. She swam trials of 4x50 and 2x100 and 1x150 plus 1x50 according to this plan. Each trial assured that Jane was on course to set a new record; the race was simply a test of whether Jane could put the full plan together. In this example, Jane broke the New Zealand Open record with a swim of 2:30.92. The only variation from the plan was an increase to 10 strokes in the last 25 meters.

Thursday of each week in the speed period of training is allocated to a review of the week's time trials. Different distance trials test the swimmer's speed or their endurance or their ability to swim the proposed race plan. The whole purpose of the trial process is to expose weaknesses.

For example, are swimmers slowing down through the trial? Even at the Olympic Games this is a problem. In the men's 50-meter freestyle final at the London Games, the average speed from 15 to 25 meters was 2.23 meters per second. In the final 15 meters this had slowed by 15% to 1.93 meters per second. If this sort of drop off is a feature of Olympic swimming, it clearly needs to be part of a junior swimmer's preparation.

If a swimmer is found to be short of speed, time can be allocated in the Thursday review session to additional speed training. If the trials indicate an anaerobic fitness problem, an additional fitness session can be added. Anaerobic sessions need to be short and quite harsh. I have three favourites that I use to correct a shortage of anaerobic fitness, which are shown in the following table.

TIME TRIAL	DESCRIPTION	INTERVAL
6x50	All swum fast from a dive. In main stroke.	On a 1-min. interval
5x100	All swum fast. Keep pace even.	Long rest. On 3 mins.
3x75+25	All swum fast from a dive. In main stroke.	10 sec. between 75 and 25. On 3 mins.

Swimmers can also have difficulty holding an even stroke rhythm. The current Olympic men's 50-meter freestyle champion's stroke rhythm dropped from 0.98 seconds per stroke in the first 25 meters to 1.11 seconds per stroke in the second half. That is a big drop. When Toni Jeffs won a bronze medal in the World Cup Short Course Finals in 1992, she swam the first 25 meters with a stroke rhythm of 0.78 seconds per stroke. In the second 25 meters this had slowed to 0.86. But junior swimmers normally have stroke rhythm drop off numbers far worse than these.

Finally, the stroke count or distance per stroke can be measured. Here again even Olympic champions have problems. In the London Olympic Games men's 50-meter freestyle final, the distance per stroke of every swimmer reduced through the course of the race – some by as much as 10%. The swimmers could not hold a consistent stroke size.

If the trials show that a swimmer has failed to swim the planned number of strokes or has altered the planned stroke rhythm, then this can be practiced in the Thursday review sessions.

A critical aspect of the 10-week speed period is this constant test and correct process. As Lydiard said, "If you test something 20 times in ten weeks and take 10 corrective measures and still get the conclusion wrong, you really should consider whether you have what it takes to be a swimming coach."

Most certainly the test and correction approach to peaking for a pinnacle event has huge advantages over the "train like mad and hope" method of tapering. In this programme the pinnacle event is the culmination of 10 weeks of progressive development. The swimmer builds up to the pinnacle event rather than the arbitrary taper down after a period of intense and often dangerous training.

Friday and Sunday training sessions are set aside for easy aerobic swimming and race and stroke technique improvements. Easy aerobic swimming is included for two reasons. First, it is important to maintain the fitness gains of the season's aerobic and anaerobic periods. Fitness is not something that can be gained and forgotten. Attention needs to be given to preserving the gains. These sessions do that. Second, easy aerobic sessions allow the swimmer time to recover. The aerobic sessions on Friday and Sunday also allow time for swimmers to practice stroke technique drills and race skills such as starts, turns and underwater skills.

Stroke technique drills are important all year. However, they merit special emphasis during the speed period of the season. The single biggest difference between swimming in my era and modern swimming is the use of drills. Modern swimmers simply swim better. They are more efficient, and drills have been a major contributor to the change. For all swimmers, drills are important, but for young swimmers, they are essential because young swimmers are learning basic techniques for the first time. Getting the basics right from the beginning avoids many problems later.

Drills are also the very best form of stretching. Although my swimmers only use drills for flexibility, they have always scored well in this test at federation camps. Drills are swimming specific and avoid the danger of overstretching injuries characteristic of many dry land stretching exercises.

I use a programme of 20 drills, two or three times per week, through the speed period. Only swim 25 meters of each drill. Long distances of a single drill normally result in the drill being done badly. The following table shows the full set of drills.

DRILL NAME	DESCRIPTION
Freestyle	
Hand over back	At completion of arm stroke, swing arm across back and touch water on opposite side. Emphasize hips roll close to 180 degrees.
Thumbs-up	During arm recovery with thumbs touching side, slide thumbs up until under arms before reaching forward. Emphasize high elbows.
Janet Evans	Straight arm recovery aiming for maximum size of stroke. Arm is bent normally during the pull.
Four plus four	Four strokes done as thumbs-up followed by four strokes done as Janet Evans. Emphasize stroke size.
Chicken wings	With thumbs tucked under armpit, swim using the elbows to pull. Emphasis should be on shoulder rotation.
Bounding	Swim with head, shoulders and hips held as high as possible. Similar to water polo freestyle. Emphasize height above water.
Fists	Normal freestyle done with closed fist. Emphasize bent elbow pull under the water
DPS free	Length done in minimum number of strokes. Emphasize glide and size to reduce the number of strokes.
Backstroke	
Three-second back	Pause stroke for three seconds as each arm enters the water at top of stroke. Emphasize body roll close to 180 degrees.
Thumbs-up back	During arm recovery with thumbs touching leg and torso, slide thumbs up to chest before reaching back. Emphasize shoulder rotation.
Double arm back	Sometimes called butterfly backstroke – both arms rotating together. Emphasize bent arm pull under the water.
DPS back	Length done in minimum number of strokes. Emphasize glide and size to reduce the number of strokes.
Breaststroke	
Three kick breast	Three kicks taken to each one arm stroke. Emphasize traveling as far as possible with each kick. Reduce the number of kicks.
Fly kick breast arms	Stroke done with normal arm stroke but butterfly hips and leg kick. Emphasize high hips in the push forward for each stroke.
Delayed kick breast	Complete full arm stroke and wait three seconds before doing kick. Emphasize delay in making kick as late as possible in the stroke.
DPS breast	Length done in minimum number of strokes. Emphasize glide and size to reduce the number of strokes.
Butterfly	
Fly drills	Butterfly done as one stroke with the left arm followed by one stroke with the right arm. Emphasize maximum size and DPS each stroke.
Huegill drill	Normal butterfly pull under water with full arm recovery also done under the water. Emphasize hour glass pull.
DPS fly	Length done in minimum number of strokes. Emphasize glide and size to reduce the number of strokes.
Normal fly	Length done with same size strokes as DPS but with faster normal butterfly rhythm.

Four drills demonstrated by Saudi Arabian swimmers, Eyad Masoud and Loai Tashkandi – double arm backstroke (1), Janet Evans (2), fly kick breast arms (3) and hand over back freestyle (4).

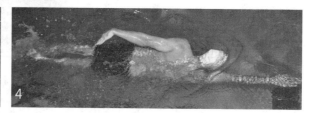

In addition to stroke drills, time needs to be allocated in the speed period of training to starts, turns and underwater technique. As with most skills good habits should be taught early in a swimmer's career. I prefer to teach simple starts and turns. Get the basics right and leave out the extravagant displays you see from some swimmers. We went through a period where swimmers were leaping into the air and jack-knifing into the pool. All that dramatic stuff looked spectacular but achieved nothing. I have been fortunate enough to coach several swimmers with fast starts. Jane Copland Pavlovich, Eyad Masoud and Joseph Skuba frequently achieved start times in the low to mid 0.5 seconds. Their fast starts were because of regular practice combined with the principle of keeping the dive simple and straight down into the pool; the emphasis was on hitting the water as fast as possible to maximize the underwater benefit rather than trying to leap out as far as possible.

Perfecting the simple things is equally important in teaching good turns. The basics are very simple. For a flip turn, get in close to the wall, flip fast and stay in a good tuck. But even simple things take practice.

What has changed in recent years is the importance of underwater butterfly kicks away from the start and turn. For example, in the men's 50-meter freestyle in the Sydney 2000 Olympic Games, the winner's underwater speed at the start was 2.80 meters per second. Twelve years later in 2012, that had increased by 12% to 3.15 meters per second. In 2017 Pavel Sankovich kicked 50 meters freestyle underwater to win the B final of the Atlanta Arena Pro Swim Series in an incredible 22.73 seconds. Because he had gone past the permitted 15 meters under the water, he was, of course, disqualified, but his swim does demonstrate the potential of good underwater technique.

Junior swimmers should be taught to fly kick away from the pool wall in every position: on their front, on their back and on their side. Once again, the simple things matter. Many swimmers have good kick technique but kick too slowly. To be successful the kicks and hip movements must be fast. The number of kicks varies, of course, with age and event. But whatever the number, both junior swimmers and mature swimmers should practice according to a predetermined formula. Practice will show what works best for each swimmer before they run out of air or speed. At the start of their careers, three or four kicks is enough. As swimmers improve and mature, the number of kicks should increase.

The transition from underwater kicks to swimming is also of critical importance. Make sure this is thoroughly practiced and drilled. The first stroke is key. The first stroke in every discipline should begin while the swimmer's head is still three or four inches under the water. The purpose of the first stroke is to lift the swimmer out of the pool and forward so that the process of swimming can begin quickly, cleanly and without interruption.

The programme described here often gets referred to as "long-distance" training. Others, less kind, use words like "garbage yardage" to portray the emphasis they believe the programme places on aerobic conditioning. However, the speed period is the most immediately important portion of the programme. This is when preparation is made to race. This is the culmination of everything that has gone before. Aerobic and anaerobic training are the athlete's preparation for the future. The speed period is the future.

During the speed period it is important to juggle and maintain the priority of several factors. The following table summarizes the seven priorities of this period of training.

QUALITY TO BE DEVELOPED	DISCUSSION
1 Preserving freshness and sharpness	This is critical. It is time to enjoy going fast. To do that swimmers need to be rested, fresh and sharp.
2 Maintaining aerobic condition	Training sessions over and above those allocated to specific tasks should involve steady aerobic swimming to maintain the base and recover from the fast speed training.
3 Developing speed	Because it is now time to go racing, training needs to develop the speed required to race well. The general conditioning has been completed. Now is time to put the fine speed in place.
4 Further developing anaerobic fitness	When a shortage of anaerobic fitness is detected, short, sharp anaerobic sets should be included to further promote anaerobic fitness. Races are also anaerobic and will further improve anaerobic fitness.
5 Developing race plans	Swimmers need to prepare and practice a race plan for their pinnacle event. This needs to include pace, stroke count and turnover – factors that can be focused on during the race.
6 Developing race techniques	Attention needs to be paid to race skills such as starts, turns and underwater work. The principle to follow in all three is to keep the teaching simple. Do the simple things well.
7 Developing stroke skills	Significant progress can be made by improved technique. Swimming better works. Use of the 20 drills detailed here will have a dramatic effect on swimmer's technique.

Eyad Masoud – Done well, good swimming looks simple, smooth and easy.

CHAPTER 8

WHAT DO THE DAILY SCHEDULES LOOK LIKE?

We have discussed the principles that should apply to the preparation of training in the aerobic, the anaerobic and speed periods. This chapter provides examples of the individual daily schedules for one week of training for each period. Two sample daily schedules are shown for each period: one for senior swimmers doing a full programme and one for junior swimmers.

The sample daily schedules for each period do not provide a complete picture of the swim training in a 24-week season. However, they do highlight the differences between periods. They also illustrate how the principles discussed in the previous chapters look in practice.

ONE WEEK OF AEROBIC TRAINING FOR SENIOR SWIMMERS SWIMMING 100 KILOMETERS

Distance Summary of Senior Aerobic Week

DAY	MORNING	DISTANCE (KM)	AFTERNOON	DISTANCE (KM)
Monday	Mixed	6	Medley	8
Tuesday	Kick	7.5	Long Main Set	10
Wednesday	Mixed	8	Mixed	6
Thursday	Kick	7.5	Long Main Set	10
Friday	Mixed	6	Medley	8
Saturday	Long Main Set	10	Stroke Correction	5
Sunday	Mixed	8	–	–
Total (km)	AM = 53		PM = 47	Week = 100

Monday AM – 6,000 Mixed

Warm-up	1000	Kick, with fins
Swim	5x200	Done as: 1. Butterfly 2. Backstroke 3. Breaststroke 4. Freestyle 5. Individual medley
Kick	1000	Kick, with fins
Swim	10x100	Freestyle – 15-second interval
Kick	1000	Done as: 1. 200 breaststroke kick 2. No fins
Swim	20x50	Done as: 1. 5x50 each stroke

Monday PM – 8000 Individual Medley

Set 1 – No fins	1. 1000 freestyle pull 2. 700 backstroke swim 3. 200 breaststroke swim 4. 100 breaststroke kick
Set 2 – With fins	1. 1000 butterfly/butterfly drills 2. 700 freestyle kick 3. 200 backstroke kick 4. 100 butterfly kick
Set 3 – No fins	1. 1000 freestyle pull 2. 700 backstroke pull 3. 200 breaststroke swim 4. breaststroke kick
Set 4 – With fins	1. 1000 individual medley 2. 700 freestyle kick 3. 200 backstroke kick 4. 100 butterfly kick

Tuesday AM – 7500 Kick

Warm-up	1500	Swim, no fins
	1000	Kick, with fins
Swim	5x100	Butterfly
Kick	200	Butterfly, no fins
	300	Butterfly, with fins
Swim	5x100	Backstroke
Kick	200	Backstroke, no fins
	300	Backstroke, with fins
Swim	5x100	Breaststroke
Kick	500	Breaststroke
Swim	5x100	Freestyle
Kick	200	Freestyle, no fins
	300	Freestyle, with fins
Cool-down	1000	Swim, with fins

Tuesday PM – 10,000 Long Main Set Programme

Warm-up	1000	Kick, with fins
	1000	Swim, no fins
Main set	4x500	Freestyle swim
	4x500	Freestyle pull
	1x500	Breaststroke swim
	2x500	Backstroke swim
	1x500	Backstroke pull
Cool-down	1000	Kick, with fins
	1000	Swim, with fins

Wednesday AM – 8000 Mixed

Warm-up	1000	Kick, with fins
	1000	Swim, no fins
	1000	Pull, no fins
Main set	32x100	Individual medley – 20-second interval
Cool-down	1000	Kick, with fins
	800	Swim, with fins

Wednesday PM – 6000 Mixed

Warm-up	500	Kick, with fins
	500	Swim, no fins
	500	Pull, no fins
Main set	1500	Butterfly/Butterfly drills, with fins
	1500	Freestyle, pull
Cool-down	1000	Kick, with fins
	500	Swim, with fins

Thursday AM – 7500 Kick

Warm-up	1500	Swim, no fins
	1500	Pull, no fins
Main set	3000	Kick, with fins
	500	Kick, no fins
Cool-down	1000	Swim, with fins

Thursday PM – 10,000 Long, Main Set Programme

Warm-up	1000	Kick, with fins
	1000	Swim, no fins
Main set	2x1500	Swim, freestyle
	1x1500	Pull, freestyle
	1x1500	Swim, backstroke
Cool-down	1000	Kick, with fins
	1000	Swim, with fins

Friday AM – 6000 Mixed

Swim	1000	
Kick	1500	With fins
Pull	1000	
Swim	1000	Individual medley done as:
		1. 100 butterfly
		2. 200 individual medley
		3. 100 backstroke
		4. 200 individual medley
		5. 100 breaststroke
		6. 200 individual medley
		7. 100 freestyle
Kick	1500	With fins

Friday PM – 8000 Medley

Set 1	2000	Swim, freestyle, no fins
	1200	Kick, freestyle, with fins
	800	Pull, freestyle, no fins
Set 2	1400	Swim, backstroke, no fins
	800	Kick, backstroke, with fins
	400	Pull, backstroke, no fins
Set 3	800	Swim, individual medley, no fins
	400	Kick, individual medley, with fins (except breaststroke)
	200	Swim, individual medley, no fins

Saturday AM – 10,000 Long, Main Set Programme

Swim	100x100	Freestyle – 15-second recovery

Saturday PM – 5000 Stroke Correction

Warm-up	1000	Kick, with fins
	1000	Swim, no fins
Drills	500	
Stroke correction	800	
Kick	3x400	With fins, done as: 1. Freestyle 2. Backstroke 3. Butterfly
Kick	500	Breaststroke

Sunday AM – 8000 Mixed

Warm-up	2000	No fins
Swim	20x50	Freestyle, no fins
Kick	2000	With fins
Swim	20x50	Breaststroke
Pull	2000	No fins

ONE WEEK OF AEROBIC TRAINING FOR JUNIOR SWIMMERS SWIMMING 30 KILOMETERS

Distance Summary of Junior Aerobic Week

DAY	MORNING	DISTANCE (KM)	AFTERNOON	DISTANCE (KM)
Monday	–	–	Medley	4.5
Tuesday	–	–	Long main set	6
Wednesday	–	–	Mixed	4.5
Thursday	–	–	Long main set	5.5
Friday	–	–	Medley	4.5
Saturday	Long main set	5	–	–
Sunday	–	–	–	–
Total	AM = 5	PM = 25		Week = 30

Monday PM – 4500 Mixed

Warm-up	500	Kick, with fins
Swim	5x200	Done as: 1. Butterfly 2. Backstroke 3. Breaststroke 4. Freestyle 5. Individual medley
Kick	500	Kick, with fins
Swim	10x100	Freestyle – 15-second interval
Kick	500	Done as: 1. 200 breaststroke kick 2. 800 with fins
Swim	20x50	Done as: 1. 5x50 each stroke

Tuesday PM – 6000 Long, Main Set Programme

Warm-up	500	Kick, with fins
Main set	4x500	Freestyle swim
	4x500	Freestyle pull
	2x500	Backstroke swim
	1x500	Backstroke pull

Wednesday PM – 4500 Mixed

Warm-up	500	Drills, with fins
Main set	32x100	Individual medley – 15-second interval
Cool-down	800	Kick, with fins

Thursday PM – 5500 Long, Main Set Programme

Warm-up	500	Kick, with fins
Main set	2x1000	Swim, freestyle
	1x1000	Pull, freestyle
	1x1000	Swim, backstroke
Cool-down	1000	Kick, with fins

Friday AM – 4500 Mixed

Swim	1500	With fins
Drills	500	
Swim	1000	Individual medley; done as:
		1. 100 butterfly
		2. 200 individual medley
		3. 100 backstroke
		4. 200 individual medley
		5. 100 breaststroke
		6. 200 individual medley
		7. Freestyle
Kick	1500	With fins

Saturday AM – 5000 Long Main Set Programme

Kick	500	With fins
Swim	20x100	Freestyle – 15-second recovery
Kick	500	With fins
Pull	20x100	Freestyle – 15-second recovery

Our club team wins the Florida State Relay Championship – Ozzie Quevedo, Joe Skuba, Andrew Meeder and Doug Millar.

ONE WEEK OF ANAEROBIC TRAINING FOR SENIOR SWIMMERS SWIMMING 70 KILOMETERS

Distance Summary of Senior Anaerobic Week

DAY	MORNING	DISTANCE (KM)	AFTERNOON	DISTANCE (KM)
Monday	Long	5	Kick	5.5
Tuesday	Long	6	Main anaerobic set	5
Wednesday	Long	6	Short sprints	6
Thursday	Medley	6	Main anaerobic set	5
Friday	Kick	6	Mixed	5
Saturday	Main anaerobic set	5	Stroke correction	4.5
Sunday	Mixed	5	–	–
Total	AM = 39		PM = 31	Week = 70

Monday AM – 5000 Long

Warm-up	500	Swim, no fins
	500	Kick, with fins
Main set	3000	Swim, no fins
Cool-down	500	Kick, with fins
	500	Swim, with fins

Monday PM – 5500 Kick

Warm-up	1000	Swim, no fins
Main set	4x300	Kick, with fins; done as:
		1. 1x100 freestyle
		2. 1x100 backstroke
		3. 1x100 butterfly
	6x300	Kick, with fins; done as:
		1. 2x300 freestyle
		2. 2x300 backstroke
		3. 2x300 butterfly
	1000	Kick, no fins; done as:
		1. Individual medley
Cool-down	500	Swim, no fins

Tuesday AM – 6000 Long

Warm-up	500	Kick, with fins
	500	Swim, no fins
Main set	4x1000	Done as:
		1. Butterfly
		2. 3 x freestyle
Cool-down	500	Kick, with fins
	500	Swim, with fins

Tuesday PM – 5000 Main Anaerobic Set

Warm-up	500	Swim, no fins
	500	Kick, with fins
Drills	500	
Main set	6x400	Done as:
		1. 2x400 freestyle
		2. 1x400 breaststroke
		3. 1x400 Backstroke
		4. 1x400 individual medley swim
		5. 1x400 individual medley kick
Cool-down	500	Kick, with fins
	500	Swim, with fins

Wednesday AM – 6000 Long

Warm-up	500	Kick, with fins
	500	Swim, no fins
Main set	4x1000	Done as:
		1. 3 x freestyle
		2. 1xIM
Cool-down	500	Kick, with fins
	500	Swim, with fins

Wednesday PM – 6000 Short Sprints

Warm-up	1. 400	Swim, no fins
	2. 4x100	
	3. 4x50	
	1000	Kick, with fins
Drills	500	
Main set	7x15	Freestyle swim hills
	7x15	Butterfly swim hills
	7x15	Breaststroke kick hills
	7x15	Backstroke kick hills
Cool-down	1000	Kick, with fins
	1000	Swim, with fins

Thursday AM – 6000 Individual Medley

Set 1, no fins	2000	Freestyle, swim
	700	Backstroke, swim
	200	Breaststroke, swim
	100	Breaststroke, kick
Set 2, with fins	700	Freestyle, kick
	200	Backstroke, kick
	100	Butterfly, kick
Set 3, with fins	1000	Individual medley swim
	700	Freestyle, kick
	200	Backstroke, kick
	100	Butterfly, kick

Thursday PM – 5000 Main Anaerobic Set

Warm-up	500	Kick, with fins
	500	Swim, no fins
Drills	500	
Main set	45x50	Done as:
		1. 35x50 swim
		2. 10x50 kick
Cool-down	500	Kick, with fins
	500	Swim, with fins

Friday AM - 6000 Kick

Warm-up	1000	Kick, with fins
Main set	5x200	Swim, no fins; done as:
		1. 1 x butterfly, with fins
		2. 1 x backstroke
		3. 1 x breaststroke
		4. 1 x freestyle
		5. 1 x individual medley
	1000	Kick, with fins
	10x100	Swim, no fins, freestyle
	1000	Kick, with fins
	20x50	Swim, no fins, 5 x each stroke

Friday PM – 5000 Mixed

Warm-up	500	Kick, with fins
	500	Swim, no fins
Main set	5x200	Swim:
		1. 5 x individual medley
		2. 5 x breaststroke
	1000	Kick; done as:
		1. 800 with fins
		2. 200 breaststroke kick
	10x100	Swim:
		1. 5 x individual medley
		2. 5 x breaststroke
Cool-down	500	Kick, with fins
	500	Swim, with fins

Saturday AM – 5000 Main Anaerobic Set

Warm-up	500	Kick, with fins
	500	Swim, no fins
Drills	500	
Main set	16x150	Done as: 1. 12x150 swim 2. 4x150 kick
Cool-down	500	Kick, with fins
	500	Swim, with fins

Saturday PM – 4500 Stroke Correction

Warm-up	1000	Kick, with fins
	1000	Swim, no fins
Drills	500	
Main set	800	Stroke correction
Kick	3x400	With fins; done as: 1. Freestyle 2. Backstroke 3. Butterfly

Sunday AM – 5000 Mixed

Swim	1000	No fins
Kick	1000	With fins
Pull	1000	No fins
Swim	20x50	Freestyle, no fins
Swim	20x50	Breaststroke

ONE WEEK OF ANAEROBIC TRAINING FOR JUNIOR SWIMMERS SWIMMING 20 KILOMETERS

Distance Summary for Junior Anaerobic Week

DAY	MORNING	DISTANCE (KM)	AFTERNOON	DISTANCE (KM)
Monday	–	–	Long	3
Tuesday	–	–	Main anaerobic set	4.5
Wednesday	–	–	Short sprints	3
Thursday	–	–	Medley	3
Friday	–	–	Mixed	2.5
Saturday	Long main set	4.5	–	–
Sunday	–	–	–	–
Total	AM = 4.5	PM = 16		Week = 20.5

Monday PM – 3000 Mixed

Warm-up	500	Swim, with fins
Main set	2000	Swim, no fins
Cool-down	500	Kick, with fins

Tuesday PM – 4500 Main Anaerobic Set

Warm-up	500	Kick, with fins
	500	Swim, no fins
Drills	500	
Main set	6x300	Done as:
		1. 5x300 freestyle
		2. 1x300 kick
Cool-down	500	Kick, with fins

Wednesday PM – 3000 Short Sprints

Warm-up	500	Kick, with fins
	500	Swim, no fins
Drills	500	
Main set	7x15	Freestyle swim hills
	7x15	Butterfly swim hills
	7x15	Breaststroke kick hills
	7x15	Backstroke kick hills
Cool-down	500	Swim, with fins

Thursday PM – 3000 Individual Medley

Set 1, no fins	700	Freestyle, swim
	200	Breaststroke, swim
	100	Breaststroke, kick
Set 2, with fins	700	Freestyle, pull
	200	Backstroke, kick
	100	Butterfly, kick
Set 3, with fins	700	Freestyle, kick
	200	Backstroke, kick
	100	Butterfly, kick

Friday PM – 2500 Mixed

Warm-up	4x200	Swim: 1. 5 x individual medley 2. 5 x breaststroke
	500	Kick; done as: 1. 800 with fins 2. 200 breaststroke kick
Main set	7x100	Swim: 1. 5 x individual medley 2. 5 x breaststroke
Cool-down	500	Kick, with fans

Saturday AM – 4500 Main Anaerobic Set

Warm-up	500	Kick, with fins
	500	Swim, no fins
Drills	500	
Main set	45x50	Done as:
		1. 35x50 swim
		2. 10x50 kick
Cool-down	500	Kick, with fins

ONE WEEK OF SPEED TRAINING FOR SENIOR SWIMMERS SWIMMING 50 KILOMETERS

Distance Summary of Senior Speed Week

DAY	MORNING	DISTANCE (KM)	AFTERNOON	DISTANCE (KM)
Monday	Mixed	3.5	Sprints	4.5
Tuesday	Mixed	3.5	Fartlek	4.5
Wednesday	Mixed	3.5	Time trial	4
Thursday	Mixed	3.5	Review	4
Friday	–	–	Mixed	6
Saturday	Time trial	4	Stroke correction	3
Sunday	Mixed	6	–	–
Total	AM = 24		PM = 26	Week = 50

Monday AM – 3500 Mixed

Main set	1500	Freestyle swim
	500	Kick
	10x100	Swim, easy
	5x100	Kick, easy

Monday PM – 4500 Sprints

Warm-up	1. 400	Swim
	2. 4x100	
	3. 4x50	
	500	Kick, no fins
Drills	500	
Main set	20x25	Sprints swim
	250	Easy recovery between
	10x25	Sprint kick
Cool-down	1000	Kick, with fins
	500	Swim, with fins

Tuesday AM – 3500 Mixed

Main set	1500	Freestyle swim
	500	Kick
	10x100	Swim, easy
	5x100	Kick, easy

Tuesday PM – 4500 Fartlek

Warm-up	1. 400	Swim
	2. 4x400	
	3. 4x50	
	500	Kick, no fins
Main set	1500	Fartlek – Freestyle swim
	500	Fartlek – Individual medley kick
Cool-down	500	Kick, no fins
	500	Swim, with fins

Wednesday AM – 3500 Mixed

Main set	1500	Freestyle swim
	500	Kick
	5x200	Swim, easy
	2x200	Kick, easy

Wednesday PM – 4000 Time Trial

Warm-up	1. 400	Swim
	2. 4x100	
	3. 4x50	
	500	Kick, no fins
Drills	500	
Main set	2x100	Time trial, one dive, one turn
Cool-down	1000	Kick, with fins
	750	Swim, with fins

Thursday AM – 3500 Mixed

Main set	1500	Freestyle swim
	500	Kick
	20x50	Swim, easy
	10x50	Kick, easy

Thursday PM – 4000 Review

Warm-up	1. 400	Swim
	2. 4x100	
	3. 4x50	
	500	Kick, no fins
Drills	500	
Main set	5x100	Fast, with 100 easy between each 100
Cool-down	500	Swim, with fins
	500	Kick, with fins

Friday AM – Rest

Friday PM – 6000 Mixed

Warm-up	1. 400	Swim
	2. 4x100	
	3. 4x50	
	500	Kick, no fins
Main set	1. 400	1. Free
	2. 200	2. IM
	3. 100	3. Fly
	4. 50	4. Fly/Back
	1. 400	1. Free
	2. 200	2. IM
	3. 100	3. Back
	4. 50	4. Back/Breast
	1. 400	1. Free
	2. 200	2. IM
	3. 100	3. Breast
	4. 50	4. Breast/Free
	1. 400	1. Free
	2. 200	2. IM
	3. 100	3. Free
	4. 50	4. Free/Fly
	10x50	Kick, easy
Cool-down	1000	Kick, with fins

Saturday AM – 4000 Time Trial

Warm-up	1. 400	Swim
	2. 4x100	
	3. 4x50	
	500	Kick, no fins
Drills	500	
Main set	150 and 50	Time trial
Warm-down	1000	Kick, with fins
	500	Swim, with fins

Saturday PM – 3000 Stroke Correction

Warm-up	1. 400	Swim
	2. 4x100	
	3. 4x50	
	500	Kick, no fins
Drills	500	
Main set	500	Stroke correction
Kick	500	No fins

Sunday AM – 6000 Mixed

Swim	1500	
Kick	1500	With fins
Swim	20x50	With fins
Swim	20x50	Done as:
		1. 5x25 each stroke
Cool-down	500	Swim
	500	Kick, no fins

ONE WEEK OF SPEED TRAINING FOR JUNIOR SWIMMERS SWIMMING 15 KILOMETERS

Distance Summary of Junior Aerobic Week

DAY	MORNING	DISTANCE (KM)	AFTERNOON	DISTANCE (KM)
Monday	-	-	Sprints	2
Tuesday	-	-	Mixed	3
Wednesday	-	-	Time trial	2.5
Thursday	-	-	Review	2.5
Friday	-	-	Fartlek	3
Saturday	Time Trial	2	-	-
Sunday	-	-	-	-
Total	AM = 2	PM = 13		Week = 15

Monday PM – 2000 Sprints

Warm-up	1. 200	Swim
	2. 2x100	
	3. 2x50	
	250	Kick, no fins
Drills	500	
Main set	10x25	Sprints swim
	150	Easy recovery between
	4x25	Sprint kick
Cool-down	250	Kick, with fins

Tuesday PM – 3000 Mixed

Main set	1000	Freestyle swim
	500	Kick
	20x50	Swim, easy
	10x50	Kick, easy

Wednesday PM – 2500 Time Trial

Warm-up	1. 200	Swim
	2. 2x100	
	3. 2x50	
	500	Kick, no fins
Drills	500	
Main set	2x100	Time trial, one drive, one turn
Cool-down	250	Kick, with fins
	250	Swim, with fins

Thursday PM – 2500 Review

Warm-up	1. 200	Swim
	2. 2x100	
	3. 2x50	
	500	Kick, no fins
Drills	500	
Main set	6x50	Fast, with 50 easy between each 50
Cool-down	250	Swim, with fins
	250	Kick, with fins

Friday PM – 3000 Fartlek

Warm-up	1. 200	Swim
	2. 2x100	
	3. 2x50	
	500	Kick, no fins
Main set	1000	Fartlek – Freestyle swim
	500	Fartlek – Individual medley kick
Cool-down	250	Kick, no fins
	250	Swim, with fins

Saturday AM – 2000 Time Trial

Warm-up	1. 200	Swim
	2. 2x100	
	3. 2x50	
	250	Kick, no fins
Drills	500	
Main set	1x200	Time trial
Cool-down	250	Swim, with fins

Ozzie Quevedo begins a day's work. Ozzie is currently the assistant swimming coach at Florida State University.

Another good butterfly swimmer, Eyad Masoud, settles into training at the British International School Pool in Jeddah, Saudi Arabia.

CHAPTER 9

HOW FAR SHOULD I SWIM?

We have discussed the physical benefits that accrue because of swimming good aerobic distances – benefits to heart, arteries, veins and capillaries. The question of what is meant by a "good aerobic distance" is, of course, key. How far does a swimmer have to swim in order to secure these physiological changes?

It is entirely possible to get hung up over distance. I know of swimmers and coaches who are obsessed with reaching a predetermined distance each week. One runner was so single minded about running 120 miles each week that she never had time to do the anaerobic and speed training properly. As a result, she never achieved the race results her application deserved. So beware, mileage can be addictive. Remember that while distance may be an important measure of each week's training, it is only one measure. What is done within the mileage is equally important.

Having said that; not enough mileage can also be a problem. When I arrived in Saudi Arabia the national team swimmers were training about 15 kilometers a week – and that was on a good week. Now I don't care who you are or what talent you have, 15 kilometers a week is not enough to compete at world class level, no matter what the content of the 15 kilometers might be. International swimming, in an aerobically-based programme, requires a minimum of between 60 kilometers and 100 kilometers a week. Which means that for young swimmers, part of a coach's job is to gradually nurture their fitness and strength from a few kilometers a week when they are young to big distances in their late teens and twenties.

The following table shows the progress in distance of one swimmer, Jane Copland Pavlovich, from learning to swim through to a senior New Zealand champion, record holder and representative. The tables show the average kilometers per week swum in each aerobic build-up in the anaerobic weeks and in the speed work portion of the season. The rate at which Jane increased the mileage content of her training is about as fast as I would ever recommend. She was incredibly tough and handled the additional work each season. I certainly would never suggest faster progress in distance than this example. For many swimmers a slower, more cautious build-up would be wise. Remember, too, that this example is a female swimmer. Girls tend to mature earlier and more quickly than boys and therefore appear to be able to handle longer distances at a younger age. Boys are normally one or two years behind in this sort of comparison.

The data covers the swimming done in the seven years, 14 seasons between the ages of 12 and 18 years. At the age of 18, Jane began swimming at Washington State University, and I lost track of her mileages. The numbers shown are average kilometers per week. Over the seven years and through the three training periods of aerobic, anaerobic and speed training, Jane totaled 16,813 kilometers for a career average weekly distance of 50.64 kilometers.

AGE	BUILD-UP (KM PER WEEK)	ANAEROBIC (KM PER WEEK)	SPEED (KM PER WEEK)	SEASON (KM PER WEEK)
12	25	20	20	23.86
12	39	35	21	31.36
13	57	46	26	38.86
13	57	68	29	44.21
14	35	30	19	24.20
14	68	74	33	53.47
15	63	41	19	35.64
15	94	67	50	65.40
16	92	68	41	62.77
16	98	71	35	64.71
17	100	65	32	60.34
17	99	76	29	72.41
18	91	79	29	62.79
18	100	79	34	66.47

Graphing the data for each training period helps provide clarity and suggests target distances that swimmers at various ages might aim for as they build towards a full adult programme. The first graph shows the weekly aerobic build-up distances swum in seven years, 14 seasons between the ages of 12 and 18.

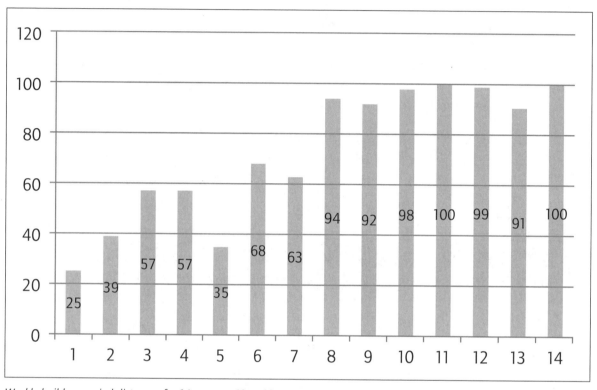

Weekly build-up period distances for 14 seasons, 12 to 18 years

Chapter 4 includes a table of minimum distances that should be swum in the build-up aerobic period. While achieving the recommended minimum distances is important, it is also wise to observe some limits. The following weekly distances are the maximum distances young swimmers should attempt in the aerobic build-up period at various ages beginning at 12 for girls and 14 for boys.

AGE (GIRLS)	AGE (BOYS)	BUILD-UP MAXIMUM WEEKLY DISTANCE (KM)
12	14	30
13	15	40
14	16	50
15	17	60
16	18	70
17	19	90
18	20	100

The second graph plots the distances swum in the anaerobic weeks. The distance, of course, drops from that swum during the aerobic build-up. The greater speed expected in the anaerobic period requires a drop in distance. Remember, "You can't run around the Waitakere Ranges and a four-minute mile at the same time." In this example, I increased Jane's anaerobic distance in season four too quickly. As you can see in the following season five, I had to reduce the distance to just 30 kilometers per week to avoid early burnout. In the next season six, I again went up to 74 kilometers and again had to drop back in season seven to 41 kilometers. Trying to combine anaerobic intensity with big mileage volumes does not work – especially in young swimmers.

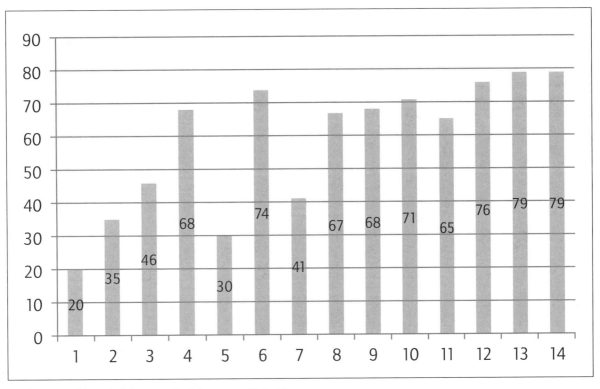

Weekly anaerobic period distances for 14 seasons, 12 to 18 years

The following weekly distances are the maximum young swimmers should attempt in the anaerobic period at various ages beginning at 12 for girls and 14 for boys.

AGE (GIRLS)	AGE (BOYS)	ANAEROBIC MAXIMUM WEEKLY DISTANCE (KM)
12	14	20
13	15	30
14	16	40
15	17	40
16	18	50
17	19	60
18	20	70

The third graph plots the distances Jane swam during the 10-week speed period. The distance swum each week now drops sharply as the importance of time trials and speed becomes paramount. However, sufficient distance needs to be included to avoid losing the gains in aerobic fitness built up earlier in the season, but distance is less important.

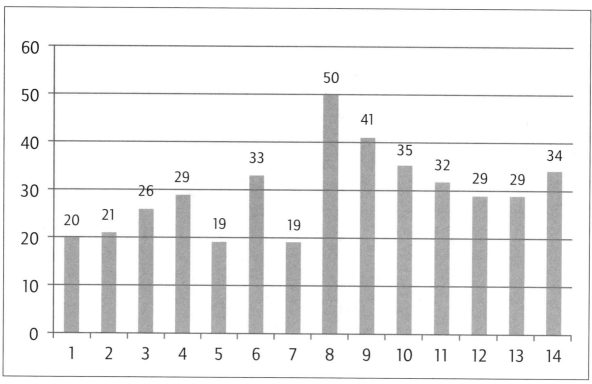

Weekly speed period distances for 14 seasons, 12 to 18 years

The following weekly distances are the maximum swimmers should attempt in the speed period of training at various ages beginning at 12 for girls and 14 for boys.

AGE (GIRLS)	AGE (BOYS)	SPEED MAXIMUM WEEKLY DISTANCE (KM)
12	14	15
13	15	20
14	16	30
15	17	30
16	18	40
17	19	50
18	20	50

Over a full season of 24 weeks, the final graph plots the total average distance swum each week. This figure is an average of the distances swum in the aerobic, the anaerobic and the speed weeks combined. As you can see in this example, as a senior swimmer, Jane averaged around 65 kilometers a week – 1,690 kilometers a season, 3,380 kilometres a year. Senior swimmers using an aerobic training programme accept that between 3,000 and 3,500 kilometers is their expected normal annual training volume.

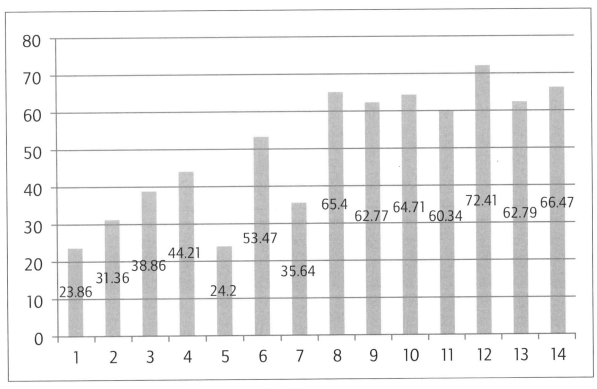

Weekly consolidated season distances for 14 seasons, 12 to 18 years

From these recommendations, the final table in this section consolidates all three periods and shows the average and total mileages recommended for each age group. For example, an age group female swimmer at 12 and a boy at 14 could swim, without risk, about 22 kilometers a week, 1,060 kilometers a year. Each year, this distance can be increased until at 17 for girls and 19 for boys the swimmers should be capable of the adult training volume of 68 kilometers a week average and 3,280 kilometers annual mileage. At 18 for girls and 20 for boys, the maximum weekly average distance of 74 kilometers per week and 3,552 per year is reached.

AGE (GIRLS)	AGE (BOYS)	BUILD-UP (KM)	ANAEROBIC (KM)	SPEED PERIOD (KM)	AVG. SEASON (KM)	SEASON TOTAL (KM)	ANNUAL TOTAL (KM)
12	14	30	20	15	22	530	1060
13	15	40	30	20	30	720	1440
14	16	50	40	30	40	960	1920
15	17	60	40	30	44	1060	2120
16	18	70	50	40	54	1300	2600
17	19	90	60	50	68	1640	3280
18	20	100	70	50	74	1776	3552

It is important to stress again that the data used in this distance chapter are based on the career of an extremely tough young swimmer, so caution is needed. When it comes to increasing the distance swum, the figures shown are maximums. They are a guide to what can be achieved. There is no harm in taking an extra year to reach a mature swimmer's training volume. There is no harm in never reaching the full 3,552 kilometers in a year. Plenty of very good swimmers have trained using an aerobic-based programme of a lot less than 3,552 kilometers.

Toni Jeffs and Nichola Chellingworth were national open champions, record holders and representatives. Both swam a balanced aerobic training programme. However, their annual mileage totals were always well short of 3,552 kilometers. Both swimmers normally swam around 2,500 kilometers a year. So the moral really is, as a swimmer gets older, increase the distance swum but exercise caution.

Look for signs of overtraining and ease back if they occur. Recognize that any increase in distance has the potential to cause problems such as poor performance, high levels of fatigue, disturbed sleep, irritability and muscle soreness. It is important to understand that at the same time as swimmers are being asked to swim farther they are also looking to swim faster. And that is dangerous. In Laurel MacKinnon's Queensland study, elite swimmers were asked to increase their training volume by 10% each week for four weeks while maintaining the same training intensity. One-third of the swimmers demonstrated a variety of fatigue symptoms. The conclusion was obvious but is so often overlooked. Athletes training at high levels of physical stress cannot tolerate sudden or large increases in training distance for more than a very short period without showing symptoms of overtraining. In elite swimmers, the problem can be serious. In junior swimmers, the problem is terminal.

Syrian swimmer, Eyad Masoud, lives and trains in Jeddah, Saudi Arabia. Anyone wanting to experience how difficult a swimmer's life can be needs to live in this man's shoes for a day. Because of his nationality, he is not able to compete for the country he has lived in since he was three years old, he is barred from most pools, and he is refused entry into many meets because he is Syrian. Yet, on his own, he swims 60 kilometers a week and has personal best times of 54.15 100 LCM freestyle, 24.60 50 LCM freestyle and 26.66 50 LCM butterfly. Swimming New Zealand allowed him to join the Auckland, New Zealand, Waterhole Swim Club and compete in the 2017 National Swimming Championships. The generosity of countries like New Zealand and Germany to Syrians in Eyad's position deserves our respect and our thanks.

CHAPTER 10

PATIENCE

Several years ago, at the New South Wales Championships in Sydney, I had a conversation with Gennadi Touretski, the outstanding Russian coach who guided Alexander Popov and Michael Klim to swimming fame. Touretski had just finished explaining to Michael Klim that his pre-race warm-up needed to improve. As Klim walked away, Touretski said, "Even champions need shock treatment sometimes." And then turned to me and made a comment that changed my coaching life.

"Do you know what is the single most important quality in a good coach?" he asked.

"No, what is it?" I said

Touretski answered, "Patience."

From one of the world's coaching greats, there is no greater truth than that. Even Jane, used as an example in the previous chapter, took seven years to develop from a young age group swimmer to an adult senior national champion. Success seldom comes quickly. It takes time.

Over and over again the careers of young, talented swimmers end early because coaches and parents are unable to exercise patience. When coaches and parents behave badly, swimmers suffer and leave the sport early.

In this chapter I will describe events that have happened to swimmers that illustrate a lack of patience – of what not to do. Although the mistakes made in each story are different, adults unable to exercise patience is a common theme. Parents, especially, need to offer support but avoid control, have a close interest but leave their notebook of times and splits at home; they need to behave well. I am certain most of us know what that means. Here are some examples of what not to do.

THE BRIBE

At 12 years old, Jane used to compete with a girl who attended the same school. At the Wellington Short Course Championships, I was standing behind Jane's friend and her mother. They clearly were unaware of my presence because I overheard the mother say to her daughter, "If you beat Jane today, I will buy you a bike on the way home."

There is no place for that sort of bribe in the development of a young swimmer. I know of several parents who offer cash payments for every personal best time. The message sent by the bribe of a bike or a cash payment is bad. These parents are teaching their children that the only effort worth making is an effort that is paid for. That morality will never be successful in sport. I have never heard a highly paid professional sports person admit to swimming or running or playing for money. They compete for the satisfaction of doing well. And then they get paid.

Incidentally, a short time after this incident, I was telling the story to Pru Chapman, a 1968 New Zealand swimming Olympian. Pru had a very good national swimming champion son of her own by this stage. Her reaction to my story was, "Huh, that's different from me. I tell my son I'll take his bike off him if he doesn't win." She was joking, of course. But her reaction highlighted the scorn with which she viewed the bribe of a bike.

It will surprise no one to hear that two years later, at age 14, Jane's friend left competitive swimming.

PREMATURE EXPECTATIONS

In 1994, a 13-year-old swimmer transferred onto my team. She was a good swimmer, ranked in the top eight freestyle swimmers in New Zealand for her age. At the time I was coaching New Zealand champions Toni Jeffs, Nichola Chellingworth and Jane Copland Pavlovich. The new swimmer's father told me he wanted to develop his daughter's talent by having her train with the girls in my team. That was sensible; as role models you could do a lot worse than those three.

Then he added, in a pretty demanding tone, that both parents expected me to turn their daughter into a champion swimmer. In fact, he said, a motel close to the 2000 Sydney Olympic Pool had already been booked and paid for. In six years his daughter had better be there.

This was only six months after Sydney had been awarded the Games and already a motel had been booked in the expectation of watching their daughter compete. Wow, that seemed a bit premature. I wondered how that level of expectation expressed itself in their life at home – not well, was my guess.

The Games eventually came and went. The motel room was not needed. The swimmer had improved but not to the level required to swim in an Olympic Games. She was always swimming for someone else; she never experienced the freedom of competing for herself. The pressure of the parents' expectations was just too great.

CHANGING CLUBS

There are many good reasons for changing clubs. The ambition of a swimmer's parents is not one of them. I have already mentioned Anne. She was a very talented swimmer that left my club and eventually retired without realizing her potential.

Some people just don't travel well. In Spain, they can be found on the lookout for McDonalds or a Subway outlet; in Turkey searching the internet for the nearest Burger King; and beside the Rhine complaining about the absence of Californian chardonnay. Well Anne's mother Carolyn, was one of those. I took her and her daughter on a team to swim in the Mare Nostrum series. I have no idea why these three meets caused me so many problems with intra-team conflict over the years – they are relaxed but competitive events in some of Europe's most idyllic locations. A week before the first meet in Barcelona, Anne got sick. I wasn't sure what was wrong and so, with Carolyn, I took Anne to the doctor. He prescribed some antibiotics and told us to take the first meet carefully, but Anne should be fine for the second meet in Canet.

The day before the Barcelona meet, I told Anne I had scratched her from her longer races but had left her in the 50-meter freestyle. She could swim that event, but only if she felt up to the task. She said she wanted to swim, and I agreed. Anne swam. Her time was slower than her best but under the circumstances was a good swim – an indication of better things to come. Carolyn, however, could not handle the modest result. She carted Anne off to various tourist attractions in Barcelona that afternoon and arrived back at our apartment announcing that she had spoken to her husband and, with Anne, was going back to Florida the following morning. And that's what she did.

The rest of the team swam the other Mare Nostrum meets in Canet and Monte Carlo. By the time we got home, Carolyn had filed a formal complaint with the Florida Gold Coast Swimming Association, claiming I had neglected her daughter's ill health and had forced Anne to swim the 50-meter freestyle. It was rubbish, of course, especially when it was pointed out that the same Carolyn that was saying Anne was too sick to swim 50 meters had carted Anne around Barcelona for hours looking at tourist attractions. Carolyn's complaint also said that I had sent the sick Anne down to the shallow end of the Barcelona pool to practice turns. That lie was easily rebutted. The Barcelona pool doesn't have a shallow end; it's the same depth all over.

Florida Gold Coast dismissed Carolyn's Mare Nostrum complaint, but Anne was taken to another club. It was sad. Anne was a tremendous talent; at 12 years old she one of the best in the United States. In 2014/15 she should have been on a full scholarship to a good Division I programme in a school like Auburn, Texas, Stanford, Florida or Georgia. Instead, she dropped out of the Florida Atlantic University swim team in Boca Raton. Anne had the potential to swim for her country but never would. That can be the price young swimmers pay when parents behave badly.

MY CHILD MUST WIN SYNDROME

One mother was responsible for recording the results of our club's swimmers. About six months after a provincial championship, I asked for a report on the championship results. I recognized an error in the report. Toni Jeffs was correctly shown as winning the woman's 50-meter and 100-meter freestyle. However, I did not recognize the name of the swimmers shown in second and third; they were from another club. That was strange because I knew that the recorder's daughter had been second in both races. In fact, it was the first time her daughter had been beaten by Toni. I called the recorder and asked her to check the results because her daughter's swims seemed to be missing. Two months later I had not received a reply, so I rang to see if the result had been corrected. I will never forget her answer: "No," she said, "I remember those races clearly, and my daughter never swam." Would you believe it? History was changed because a mother could not bear the thought of her daughter being beaten. To this day, I would imagine, those results remain a fiction in provincial swimming history.

There is, of course, nothing wrong with parents wanting their children to do well. But there is a line that when crossed hurts those they seek to protect. This swimmer's mother crossed that line.

OBSESSIVE CONTROL

I have experienced two superstars of parents with control problems whose behavior has eventually ended their children's participation in sport.

Linda was on the committee of my Florida club. She complained about everything; nothing was good enough. While I was there, Ozzie Quevedo broke the masters world records for 50-meter and 100-meter butterfly. Obviously, I gave the swims prominent mention in the club newsletter. At the next board meeting, Linda dismissively said, "You're not taking credit for that are you?" As she was speaking, I noticed Ozzie walking into the pool. I called him over and asked if the training he had done with the club had helped his world record swims. "Of course it did," he said. Linda never forgave me for that well-earned put down.

She bombarded club members, the club committee and my extended family with emails, accusing me of all sorts of bad behaviour. She claimed financial indiscretions that never happened and were proven false. To this day, I have no idea why. Her children seemed happy and were making good progress. The club was a thriving, growing community of swimmers, from an Olympic Gold medallist to juniors who were learning to kick with kickboards.

Things got worse when I discovered Linda had asked the club to invoice her boy's training fees as a single amount and call it a gym membership. I investigated further and discovered she was claiming the cost back from her employer who offered free gym memberships to the staff as a corporate perk. I told the employer as I was not happy to be accused of financial mismanagement, only to find that my accuser was defrauding her employer with invoices from my coaching programme. Linda was fired from her job and left the swimming club.

With that history, imagine how I felt when I read the following headline in the May 19, 2014, Boca News: "Made In USA Founder, Jailed." Evidently Linda had fallen out with and had left her husband. She visited the family home while he was out and removed two bags of his belongings and took them to her car. Then, according to the report, Linda "came back into the house and took a 12-pack of Michelob beer" that she broke and poured over her ex-husband's possessions in the driveway. Afterwards, the report said, Linda was found by police in Boca Raton, Florida, and turned over to cops in Delray Beach.

That has to be karma or as a committee member from the Florida club said to me in an email on the subject: "Four greatest words in the English language: I told you so."

My pool in Delray Beach, Florida, a lovely facility

MY CHILD CAN DO NO WRONG

This attitude of "my child can do no wrong" can also cause hurt and end a promising swimming career. Probably the best and certainly the hardest working parent volunteer I've ever seen was on the committee of my club in the US Virgin Islands. He was a senior executive in a large international company. How he managed to find the hours he worked for the club was beyond belief. He was also a very courageous man; he won an award for walking into an oil refinery fire and turning off a leaking valve.

You may be asking, how could such a man cause a problem? Well, his daughter was a very good swimmer and a huge amount of fun to have on the team; she was bright, funny, rebellious, hardworking, all the qualities I enjoy being around. But she misbehaved during an overseas trip to Europe, and I decided some discipline was necessary. I banned her from the next team trip to a meet in Kingston, Jamaica. The father took that badly and conducted a pretty vicious campaign to have me removed from the club. That failed, and he ended up leaving the club. However, during the turmoil, one consistent theme repeated frequently in his many emails was that I was destroying his family. His daughter's swimming career failed to survive the turmoil. Everything about this episode was incredibly sad. The involvement of an excellent administrator and a good swimmer ended because a parent failed to understand the importance of discipline. He had a wonderful daughter who made a mistake and was suspended for one meet. His reaction was the cause of far greater harm, as so often happens.

NOTHING IS EVER GOOD ENOUGH

William was one of New Zealand's best junior swimmers. At age 14, he qualified to swim in the New Zealand Open Championships. He worked hard and was rewarded with provincial records and championships. A successful senior career seemed certain, but, sadly, William had a father who ended the dream. William's father had a notebook and recorded the times and splits of every race swum by his son. He kept a note of what his son ate, how long he slept and the progress of his son's dry land training. The detail was stunning – more than I knew and way over the top. His son may have survived his father's attention, but what he could not survive was that nothing was ever good enough.

If William won a race, the time he swam would be questioned. If he broke a record but lost to a senior swimmer, that was cause for censure. If William won and broke a record the splits, stroke count and stroke tempo would be examined, and weaknesses debated on the way home. I suggested to the father that a more positive approach may be better. Not at all, I was told; someone like William needed to be pushed, needed to be kept on his toes.

It didn't work. Shortly after finishing high school, at age 17, William retired, fed up with the whole thing. The day he stopped must have been the most liberating of his life.

WEST AUCKLAND AQUATICS

In terms of the destruction that can be caused to talented young swimmers' careers and to swimming clubs, the events at West Auckland Aquatics are without rival.

In 2015, Swimming New Zealand terminated the membership of West Auckland Aquatics. I was told that the termination of the club was the first time in Swimming New Zealand's 130-year history that a club had been expelled. Whenever something this unusual and important occurs, there are lessons to be learned. Here is what happened.

WEST AUCKLAND AQUATICS SEQUENCE OF EVENTS

- West Auckland Aquatics (WAQ) employed me as the club's head coach on April 12, 2010.

- From June 2 through July 10, 2015, I attended the Mare Nostrum series of meets in Europe with a WAQ swimmer. During this time, I arranged for an ex-national coach to coach my West Auckland team.

- On July 11, 2015, I returned to New Zealand. Unfortunately, I spent some time in the hospital afterward, being treated for a foot infection. During that time, a WAQ parent and the relief coach visited me. The parent had a 13-year-old daughter who was a good swimmer and ranked in the top 10 for her age in New Zealand.

- During the hospital visit they proposed that a new club should be formed to take over the West Wave Aquatic Centre lane space currently used by WAQ.

- They said that they had in mind forming a new club with joint head coaches. They claimed this would benefit the swimming of members. The existing three clubs using the West Wave Pool would merge their members into the newly formed super club. I advised them that I thought the suggestion wasn't in the best interest of swimming in west Auckland. The three existing clubs had different areas of specialty and worked well together. They were annoyed that I rejected their plan and effectively stopped communicating with me.

- On July 28, 2015, the parent met with the CEO of the West Wave Aquatic Centre and proposed replacing WAQ with a new "super club" with the replacement coach as the sole coach. I was now excluded from the plan. West Wave Aquatic Centre declined the approach.

- On August 4, 2015, the parent met the CEO of the Auckland Swimming Association and put the same "super club" proposal to him. The Auckland Swimming Association declined the plan. Her plan had been rejected for a third time.

- On September 14, 2015, the WAQ annual general meeting was held, and the parent was appointed unopposed as president. I was appointed a committee member, one of eight.

- On October 15, 2015, the new president proposed that the committee employ the replacement coach as co-head coach. Having been unable to form a super club, she appeared intent on converting WAQ into what she wanted from the inside. The committee deferred any discussion on the proposal.

- On October 22, 2015, a special general meeting was called to consider a motion of no confidence in the president. The meeting was never held, and the motion never considered.

- The president's decision to ignore the members' constitutional request for a special general meeting was a significant event; effectively, WAQ was now controlled by the president.

- The WAQ committee was reduced by four resignations and was now an unconstitutional four members.

- On November 5, 2015, Swimming New Zealand (SNZ) called a meeting with the SNZ chairman, the CEO and me to discuss the breakdown of WAQ management. I explained that the president's family had been asked to leave or refused entry to three previous clubs. A pattern was emerging at WAQ. SNZ said they would consider the position and advise me of what action they proposed to take.

- On November 16, 2015, SNZ called a second meeting, this time with all four remaining WAQ committee members. At the meeting, SNZ proposed a form of SNZ statutory management of WAQ on the condition that all four current committee members resign and do not stand for the WAQ committee again for five years. The president and one committee member declined the SNZ offer. This effectively sealed the fate of WAQ as a member club of SNZ.

- On November 19, 2015, West Wave Pool suspended WAQ lane space, effective from November 22. SNZ also suspended WAQ membership for bringing the sport into disrepute.

- On December 3, 2015, the president dismissed me as head coach without membership or committee consent. At the same time, the president appointed the replacement coach to coach WAQ swimmers in the Massey High School pool. It took her less than 12 hours to do so.

- On December 9 and 14, 2015, the president submitted a club "rescue" plan to SNZ. This was rejected by SNZ, and WAQ members were advised that WAQ membership of SNZ was permanently terminated.

- The president's daughter swam her first recorded race on August 16, 2011, at age eight: 100 IM in 1:54.31. Since then, she has competed in 161 races. However, following the political drama of 2015, her participation in 2016 was only three meets and eight races. She has not competed at all in 2017 or 2018. All that destruction seems to have resulted in another early teen dropout. All that destruction for nothing.

CHAPTER 11

ROLE OF THE COACH

In his book, *Heroes and Sparrows*, Roger Robinson describes the history and role of a coach. His essay forms the basis of my coaching philosophy. Roger provides everything that is important in a coaching mission statement.

Roger begins by highlighting the extremes of status given to the position of coach. In Victorian England the coach was merely an assistant and a masseur. At the same time, in Japan, coaches were revered as spiritual leaders and masters. The masseur and master were extremes of status in the history of the sports coach. On one hand a servant and on the other a godlike leader.

Roger then goes back to Ancient Greece to look at the even earlier role of the coach. Fascinating in this extract is the description of Greek training. It was, he says, based on a four-day cycle: Day 1 was for "Preparation"; day 2 was "Concentration"; day 3, "Relaxation"; and day 4, "Moderation". That is not far away from modern training programmes. Those Greeks, it seems, knew a thing or two about sport.

Most importantly, Roger highlights the status of coaches in Greek life. They were powerful and respected. Coaches were truly academics – engaged in an important area of learning and culture. In modern swimming there is much to that thought. The success of American swimming is closely linked to the respect given to their coaches. When I began coaching in the United States, I could not believe the regard given to my position. The failure of swimming in other regimes often stems from administrations that undervalue the role of the coach. In New Zealand and Saudi Arabia, I have heard both national CEOs tear apart the nation's coaches. They had no idea of the damage their criticism caused.

Finally, Roger sets out his definition, and mine, of the role of the coach. The importance of his description cannot be overstated. It sets out perfectly the scope, responsibilities and the limitations of a coach. What is written here should be a compulsory unit of learning in every coaching course. Here is how Roger brilliantly describes the role of the coach.

Our main training pool at the Beeston Hill Fitness Centre in the US Virgin Islands

"To define the coach's role, I should like to be dryly academic for a moment and define the word itself. Kotcz is a small place in Hungary, between Raab and Buda, which gave its name back in the fourteenth century to a special kind of vehicle, a 'kotczi-wagon' or 'kotczi-car', used for passengers on the rugged local roads. The term passed across to England after a hundred years or so, and by 1556 was anglicised as 'coach'. 'Come, my coach,' calls Ophelia in Hamlet, and she was a lady who could certainly have used help with her swimming.

So a coach is someone with whom you travel, who is a means of conveying the student or athlete along a rough road to a difficult destination. There is a moral in the dry dust of the dictionary. If we think of coaching as a means of travel, we may perceive more clearly both the importance and the limits of the coach's role. The coach has indispensable functions: to instruct, to motivate and to inculcate strategy, especially that long-term strategy which no young competitor can know by instinct. The coach should also observe clearly defined limits: not to intrude into the ultimate aloneness of the competitor nor to diminish the essentially individual satisfaction of sporting achievement. The coach's achievement and satisfaction are equally real, equally valid, but different. The means of travel is not the traveller.

As coaches gain more confidence in their status, and as more weight is given to individual fulfilment as against the team's, or worse, the coach's success, so we may hope that the proper role of the coach will be acknowledged. As a vehicle, as the essential means of transport along the high road, both for the growth of the individual engaged in sport and for the development of the body of knowledge associated with the event, the coach has a vital and satisfying role."

I fully endorse the distinction made in this article between the athlete – the traveller – and the coach – the means of travel. I have often felt uncomfortable with coaches who said, "we did this" or "we did that" or who congratulated me when one of our team swam well. The swimmer had done well. I sat on the side of the pool and watched. Yet, there was a common purpose, a shared experience that I could not define until along came Roger's brilliant definition – the coach is the means of travel, the athlete is the traveller. It is their journey.

Failing to understand this concept and putting limits on our intrusion into the athlete's world is a source of many problems that end up causing the sport's appalling dropout rate.

Pressure to get involved in swimming, to stay in swimming, to attend every training session, to increase the amount and intensity of training, to enter too many races, to achieve a personal best in every race and to win comes from a controlling amalgamation of clubs, parents and coaches. It is always in someone else's interests to see the swimmer do it and do it better, faster, longer or more.

This pressure group has forgotten it is the athlete's journey. Trophies for the club and the coach accumulating the most championship points are the most obvious. Coaches enter their best teenage swimmers in 20 races in a weekend. The swimmers go along probably because they are under orders to never question the coach's commands. But the coach should know better. Coaches let it happen because they see the journey as their journey, with no thought for the swimmers' interests or long-term goals. That is bad coaching. Good coaching places the swimmers' interests first.

The traveller and the means of travel. Athens' Olympic gold medallist, Rhi Jeffrey, and me. Rhi loved the fun of unusual hair colour. She could swim a bit as well. She had long course personal best times of 25.47 50 LCM freestyle, 55.21 100 LCM freestyle and 1:59.76 200 LCM freestyle.

CHAPTER 12

PUSHING EARLY FOR BIG RESULTS

There is a fine line between being supportive and suffocating the life out of a young athlete. The location of the line is difficult to define. Clearly for a parent like Peter Coe, the father and coach of Sebastian Coe, or a father like me, coaching my daughter Jane, the divide is in a very different place than it is for parents whose responsibility is to exercise the normal duties of being parents. Peter Coe and I had to get involved in training distances, times and splits, but as coaches, not as parents.

Parents must not act as backup coaches. A parent's notebook recording training and racing times and splits is going too far. Inevitably, that level of attention will mean the swimmer is going to receive mixed messages: one from the coach and another from the parent. When that happens the chances of a swimmer surviving are very low.

A parent's vital role is to love, house, feed, clothe, educate, care for and get their children to training. Trust the coach to manage the water side of the sport. Why? Because that is the best way to get a good result.

Several years ago, I used the expression, "If it doesn't happen naturally, it won't happen at all." As swimmers strive for faster and faster times, a coach has two options: 1) either push for even better results or 2) reassure their charge that when the time is right good things will happen. Actually, there is only one effective choice. Pushing may result in a short-term gain but inevitably leads to disappointment. Reassurance is the only option. Extreme pressure cannot force babies to climb Mount Everest. There is a time and a place.

Probably the best example of the patience required to guide a swimmer through their early development came from an incident that occurred when my daughter, Jane, was a very young toddler. Brian Cumberland, a friend of ours, had come to dinner. There was nothing subtle about Brian. He was a tough, straight and honest factory manager in the hard world of the New Zealand meat industry. On this particular night, Jane's mother, Alison, came downstairs from putting Jane to bed and said, "I'm trying to teach Jane to use the toilet. Will she ever learn?" Brian smiled and said quietly, "Don't worry, she will know what to do by the time she graduates from high school."

And isn't that the point. Good things happen in their good time. I wonder how many potential champions have been lost by coaches and parents pushing for results too soon?

The world of sport is full of advice on the merits of enduring pain and working hard. Just about everyone has heard the slogans, "No pain, no gain" and "Go hard or go home" and "When the going gets tough, the tough get going" and "Success is earned with blood, sweat, and the occasional tear." The best of the worst was posted recently on wall of the West Wave Pool in Auckland. It read, "Train insane or remain the same." Whoever invented that has no place in sport, and the pool staff who posted it on their wall should know better.

Parents and many coaches bombard young swimmers with a message of sacrifice and hurt. No one should be surprised, then, when young athletes look on their journey in sport as tough, difficult and full of pain. That's the story they have been told. And I do not agree. The emphasis on insane blood, sweat and tears promotes the likelihood of early dropout. Why stay in something that's going to cause so much hurt?

Lydiard went partway to forming my counter view with his slogan, "It's training, not straining." And then I watched some of the world best and highest paid athletes at work. Sure, they worked a full eight hours a day at their sport, but I did not detect the fanaticism of the amateur world of slogans. I saw Sir Andy Murray and Roger Federer. I watched Rory McIlroy and Sergio Garcia, Jessica Ennis-Hill and Wilma Rudolph, Katie Ledecky and Janet Evans. Yes, they practiced hard, but most of all they were professionals going about their daily business. Sport was their job, and they acted, trained and competed accordingly. Mohamed Ali said it best, as he often did, in his quote, "It's just a job. Grass grows, birds fly, waves pound the sand. I beat people up." And that is what I prefer to see in young swimmers. Not beating people up, but young athletes going about their job in and out of the pool in a dignified and professional way.

But it is not easy. Young swimmers and their parents need constant reassurance. At every swim meet they will see coaches pushing swimmers through some incredible warm-up routines. Long term, these pre-race training sessions don't work, but they look good. It is very easy for young swimmers and novice parents to think that's the way it should be done. It looks harder – it must be better. "My child is going to get more attention. That's the way good coaches should teach." I know a New Zealand coach who is a classic at putting on a stunning training pool and warm-up performance. He paces around the pool, two stopwatches working overtime, calling out instructions, demanding greater effort. His finger is permanently jammed in some coaching electric light socket.

And it is all for nothing. Worse than that, it actually causes harm. Let me use the example of two of New Zealand's best coaches to explain why. Arthur Lydiard's advice, even for young athletes, was to avoid giving training instructions on the day of a race. All that needs to be said should have been said long ago. Race day is a time for athletes to focus on their preparation free from the chatter of parents and coach. It might not look as impressive. It certainly takes a lot of self-control to quietly take a pre-race warm-up without issuing a long list of last minute instructions, but the clarity of silence is well worth the effort.

My second example is Duncan Laing, coach of double Olympic champion, Danyon Loader. I went to the World Cup Short Course Finals with the New Zealand team in 1992. Duncan was the head coach, and I was there as the coach of Toni Jeffs. On the way to Majorca we stopped for eight hours in Singapore. Duncan had arranged for the team to swim at a local university pool. I set Toni an easy 2,000-meter recovery swim plus a couple of 15-meter dives. Duncan did a small amount more with distance swimmers Danyon Loader and Philippa Langrell, but not much more. We were soon finished and on our way to lunch.

At lunch Duncan said to me, "You know, we haven't known each other for very long, and I've heard all sorts of things about your coaching, good and bad. But today I've decided you know what you are doing. On these trips I've seen coaches flog their swimmers through 5,000- or 6,000-meter sessions of sprints during stops like this and then wonder why their swimmers perform poorly at the meet. You gave Toni 2,000 meters of easy swimming. I think she will perform well."

And Duncan was right – about Toni swimming well, I mean. I still think that team is the only swimming team ever to travel from New Zealand to a world-wide competition and return with every swimmer earning a medal. Toni got a bronze in the 50-meter freestyle.

The conclusion is common sense, really. Of course, the goal is to push hard to meet and better personal challenges. Be aware, though, that there is a limit to what the young can perform. It has to be challenging, but pain is not necessary. Listen to your body. It's training, not straining.

CHAPTER 13

TOO MANY RACES

Most of us would accept that the leading example of a swimmer capable of swimming multiple events is Michael Phelps. In the Beijing Olympic Games, he entered and won eight events: the 100 butterfly, 200 butterfly, 200 IM, 400 IM, 4x100 free, 4x200 free and 4x100 medley.

The *ABC News* website recorded the accomplishment in these glowing terms:

> *Phelps already made history by matching Spitz's seven golds. Now he's one-upped Spitz's record count, cementing his place as one of the best athletes of all time.*
> *Superman. Magical. The King. The Dolphin. The Fish. The Phenomenon.*

These are just some of the words being used to describe Michael Phelps during the XXIX Summer Olympics in Beijing.

Eight events in a week is an incredible feat of application, training and commitment. By the time he swam in Beijing, Phelps had been swimming at an Olympic level for eight years. He was an internationally hardened competitor. He had to be, just to survive. He was also a grown man, age 23.

But, as it turns out, the Phelps' Beijing schedule was an easy week compared to the race programme followed by many junior swimmers. For example, in two recent meets, Mary, the swimmer mentioned earlier in this book, swam in 10 races in two days and six races in one day. Her schedule makes Phelps look positively lazy.

In case you are thinking Mary might be an unrepresentative anomaly, I looked at the 2017 New Zealand Age Group Championships and the 2017 New Zealand Junior Championships. I noted the number of races entered by every swimmer and made a record of the number of swimmers who entered and swam eight or more events. In other words, swimmers who matched or exceeded Michael Phelps' Beijing schedule. The results were stunning and are recorded in the following table.

The regions shown in the table represent different areas of New Zealand. All Stars are clubs from the lower North Island, Harlequins are clubs in the northern North Island area, Aquaknights are clubs from the centre of the North Island and Makos are clubs from the South Island. Each column in the table shows the number of swimmers entered in between eight and sixteen events.

8 EVENTS ENTERED	9 EVENTS ENTERED	10 EVENTS ENTERED	11 EVENTS ENTERED	12 EVENTS ENTERED	13 EVENTS ENTERED	14 EVENTS ENTERED	15 EVENTS ENTERED	16 EVENTS ENTERED	TOTAL EVENTS ENTERED
New Zealand 2017 Age Group Championships									
55	29	17	2	2	1	0	0	0	106
New Zealand 2017 All Stars Region Championships									
35	23	19	8	4	1	0	1	0	91
New Zealand 2017 Harlequins Region Championships									
55	36	28	16	7	2	1	0	0	145
New Zealand 2017 Aquaknights Region Championships									
45	39	31	13	6	0	0	0	0	134
New Zealand 2017 Makos Region Championships									
36	27	16	15	5	0	0	0	0	99
New Zealand 2017 Age Group and Junior Championships Combined Total									
226	154	111	54	24	4	1	1	0	575
Entries as a Percent of Total Entries									
39.3	26.7	19.4	9.3	4.2	0.7	0.2	0.2	0	100

So what does this table say? It tells us that at the combined Age Group Championships and the four regional Junior Championships a total of 575 swimmers swam in programmes the same as or harder than Phelps' Beijing programme. 349 swimmers (60.7%) had programmes with more events than Phelps. 226 swimmers (39.3%) had the same number of events as Phelps' Beijing schedule. Two swimmers came within one event (15 events) of doubling Phelps' Beijing total. The Harlequins region had the highest number of big entries with 145 swimmers. Harlequins is also New Zealand's strongest region, lending weight to the idea that the better the junior, the more he or she will be exploited.

This is a stunning number of young people flogged through an impossible number of events and facing an early exit from the sport. Phelps was a hardened international competitor. The 575 swimmers in this group are all at school, many of them at primary school.

Over-racing is not a New Zealand problem only. Swimmers everywhere are over-raced. For example, a quick look at the results of the first six finals in the 2017 Florida Gold Coast Junior Olympics showed that the 60 swimmers involved swam the following number of events.

8 & U EVENTS ENTERED	9 EVENTS ENTERED	10 EVENTS ENTERED	11 EVENTS ENTERED	12 EVENTS ENTERED	13 EVENTS ENTERED	14 EVENTS ENTERED	15 EVENTS ENTERED	16+ EVENTS ENTERED	TOTAL EVENTS ENTERED
10 and Under Age									
11	9	0	0	0	0	0	0	0	20
11 and 12 Age Group									
1	0	0	1	1	2	2	1	12	20
13 and 14 Age Group									
0	1	1	2	5	1	1	1	8	20
All Combined Age Groups									
12	10	1	3	6	3	3	2	20	60
Entries as a Percent of Total Entries									
20.0	16.7	1.7	5.0	10.0	5.0	5.0	3.3	33.3	100

Here again the numbers are stunning. 33% of the swimmers competed in 16 or more races in just three days. What Phelps took eight days to do these guys do every day – or close to it. And still administrators, coaches and parents wonder, why do we have a 70 to 80% dropout rate?

Entering this number of swims in an age group championship is bad, and it does not work. We have already discussed the failure rate of junior championship winners to progress to open national success. Yet, here are the headlines that get printed by the national federation in support of mass entries:

"The pair finished with seven gold medals each to top the individual medal count."
"Freesir-Wetzell gained two further wins today in the 10 & under division 200m medley and 100m freestyle. She was the leading medalist overall with nine medals, comprising seven gold and two silver."
"Tawa's Jack Plummer had the most medals with nine comprising four gold, four silver and a bronze with today's sole win in the 11 years 100m breaststroke."

It is ironic that at the same time as swimming administrators are acclaiming the deeds of swimmers competing in multiple events, world tennis authorities have imposed a limit on the number of tournaments players under 18 years of age can play in a year. Limiting the number of tournaments young tennis players can enter is credited with an 85% drop in premature retirements prior to age 22 and careers lasting 24% longer. Tennis players are 73% more likely to enjoy a 15-year career today compared to 1994. Certainly, swimming and tennis cannot both be right.

Short-sighted swimming administrators actually see merit in the news that a teenager has been flogged through a dozen races in two days. As for the club committees that approve these mass entries, that too is a scandal. I wonder what they think of the 18th-century custom of using 12-year-olds in British coal mines? Oh, I understand the motivation as parents flock to the clubs that exploit the most in the hope their child will be the next junior champion.

There may be some who find this opinion less than persuasive, but we should learn from the example of Johanna Konta, currently ninth in the world tennis rankings and 2017 Wimbledon Championship semi-finalist. At age 14, she was told by Australian Tennis that she "lacked the requisite talent and potential" to be a champion. Carl Lewis, who was ranked fourth in the world as a junior, was convinced. He said, "There is no correlation between a childhood success and a professional athlete."

Scientists at the American Aquatic Research Center in Boulder, Colorado, agree. In one study, they scanned the hand joints of every member of the American Olympic swimming team. Their purpose was to determine what portion of the swimmers had been early developers, on time and late developers. Evidently the rate at which the hand joints close can measure an individual's physical maturity. Of the 40 athletes tested, only two had matured early, five had matured on time and the majority were late developers.

The American scientists concluded that the probable explanation for the stunning failure of swimmers who develop early is the almost impossible burden of handling their early success, followed by the struggle to stay ahead of late developers who were such easy beats a few years earlier. Over and over again it happens: Junior winners find it impossible to handle the "shame" of being beaten by slow swimmers who used to be miles behind and often didn't even make finals. Interpreting it all as a failure on their part, the early superstars go off to the local surf patrol or to a water polo team. And that is absolutely understandable.

Take Ashley Rupapera, for example. In 2006/07 she was amazing; at 14 years old she claimed her second New Zealand national age group record with a 100IM time of 1:05.30. In the Junior Championships she entered 13 individual events, swam in 22 races and won four gold medals and two silver medals. That's 10 more races than Phelps in six fewer days. I don't know what Ashley is doing today. However, sadly, it does not include elite New Zealand swimming.

Age group championship meets are the scene of too much hurt. At the beginning of the week keen, enthusiastic, happy young people arrive full of anticipation, coached and honed to a competitive edge. Parents dash around the pool checking that their charge's start list seed times have been properly entered and locating the town's best source of pasta. Coaches patrol the pre-meet practice with all the intensity of an Olympic warm-up. International swim meet promoters would die to be able to create the nervous energy present at the beginning of your average age group championship.

By the end of the first morning's heats you can detect the mood beginning to change. The problem is 30 swimmers enter an event, eight make a final, three get medals and one wins. Potentially, there are 29 disappointed swimmers and 58 disappointed parents who can't wait to get back to the motel for their treble gin and tonic to ease the pain. It is disappointment born out of expectations set far too high.

As each day goes by, the mood darkens and deepens. An adult's most valuable skill is providing comfort to another sobbing teenager. The transformation is stunning. The tremendous high of the first morning slumps during the day; is momentarily revived at the beginning of day two, only to slump even further. By day four, all I want to do is get out of the place and make sure no swimmer ever goes back. For someone whose heart is in seeing athletes soar, junior championships are no fun at all.

Several years ago, there was a good article on the USA Junior Nationals in the magazine *Splash*. In it, USA Swimming seems to be aware that their event needed to avoid many of the problems characteristic of junior swimming in New Zealand. This is what they said:

> *"Along the way, however, many coaches and others within USA Swimming saw a disturbing trend. Instead of a whistle stop on the way to senior national and international competition the Junior nationals were embedding themselves as a destination."*

The Americans have done some good things to avoid damaging the nation's youth. First, their junior event is not a normal age group meet. There are no separate annual age groups. Everyone up to a relatively old 18 years of age can swim in the event. This avoids youth swimmers being over exposed at too young an age. Second, the qualifying standards are really tough. They reflect the "older" cut-off age. An athlete must be pretty quick just to make the cut. There is a fair chance swimmers that fast will have the experience and maturity to handle the occasion. Third, names included on the meet's list of alumni suggest their "juniors" are working as a transition between sectional and international swimming. *Splash* tells me that Gary Hall, Aaron Peirsol, Ian Crocker and Michael Phelps all swam here. That's a pretty impressive list. It appears that winning is not essential, either. For example, Phelps never won the event, but he seems to have come through unscathed.

In an earlier chapter, we discussed the distances swum by Jane Copland Pavlovich through her career from junior to international competitor. In this chapter, we have cautioned against entering swimmers in too many races and have recommended a limit for senior swimmers of 50 races in a season, 100 races a year. Junior swimmers should swim fewer races than these senior maximum numbers. The following table shows how many races Jane swam before she left New Zealand to attend Washington State University.

SEASON	AGE	NO. OF RACES	RACES PER ANNUM
1	12	16	
2	12	16	32
3	13	26	
4	13	19	45
5	14	19	
6	14	68	87
7	15	55	
8	15	42	97
9	16	46	
10	16	36	82
11	17	45	
12	17	37	82
13	18	36	
14	18	32	68

You can see how we kept the racing load quite light when Jane was young: only 32 races in her first year. In two seasons (shown in bold) the number of races exceeded the recommendation of 50 races in a season. With heats and finals, it is remarkable how quickly races can mount up. Great self-control is needed to keep the number down and avoid early career dropout. Over seven years Jane averaged 70 races each year. As a comparison I entered Olympic Gold medallists, Rhi Jeffry, in an average of 58 races each year. Fifty-second 100-meter swimmer, Joe Skuba, swam an average of 40 races a year. Remember these three swimmers were world class, adult athletes. Now let's compare their annual number of races with the race numbers swum by some junior swimmers.

You may remember the example of Mary. In chapter 2 I included a table that illustrated the path of many teenage swimmers from balanced aerobic to exploitation to struggle and dropout. The number of races swum further demonstrates the transition from care to exploitation. The table of Mary's career is repeated here, but this time the number of races swum is included in the table. As you can see, in the early stages of Mary's career, I kept her racing load down to around 40 races a year. Mary then left for a sprint-based programme. Overnight, her racing load doubled to close to 80 races. Coaches and parents should know better. You cannot just double someone's workload without consequences. The result is that Mary has entered the struggle stage and, I expect, will soon be another teenage dropout.

PHASE	YEAR	AGE	TIME	TIME	DISCUSSION	NO. OF RACES
Balanced aerobic	2011	9	54	–	A period of aerobic training and steady progress. Mary improved ahead of the goal of 3% per annum	38
	2012	10	44	1:33		38
	2013	11	40	1:25		38
	2014	12	38	1:22		37
Exploitation	2015	13	33	1:12	Mary changed clubs and quickly improved by about 7% per annum.	78
	2016	14	33	1:10		72
Struggle and dropout	2017	15	34	1.10	Mary's progress stalled. Drop-out is probably one year away.	19

Anne was the other example of a swimmer whose career moved from balanced aerobic to exploitation to struggle and dropout. Her racing programme further illustrates the point. In her early career, I entered Anne in about 30 races a year. She then left to swim in a sprint-based programme. The number of races immediately more than doubled to 70 and then doubled again to 137. The adrenaline rush of all that racing was just what her parents wanted. For Anne's swimming career, it was to prove lethal. I imagine her parents just could not understand why Anne's career began to struggle. Three years later she gave the whole thing away.

PHASE	YEAR	AGE	TIME	TIME	DISCUSSION	NO. OF RACES
Balanced aerobic	2006	10	1:33	-	A period of aerobic training and steady but not spectacular improvement. Anne improved by an average of 7% per annum in the 100 and 4% in the 200.	10
	2007	11	1:16	2.45		25
	2008	12	1:11	2.35		27
	2009	13	1:06	2.23		25
Exploitation	2010	14	1:03	2.14	Anne changed clubs and quickly dropped by about 5% per annum.	70
	2011	15	1.01	2.10		137
Struggle and dropout	2012	16	1:02	2.12	For three years Anne struggled to improve. At the end of 2014, she dropped out	87
	2013	17	1:00	2.10		70
	2014	18	1:00	2.09		67

In both cases, the exploitation characteristic of Mary and Anne's training was reflected in their competition programmes. Competition hurts. When a person gets hurt often enough, they eventually go off to do something else. The rule of thumb for a senior swimmer is a maximum of 100 races a year and for junior swimmers a lot less. Stick to that rule. Your swimmer's future probably depends on it.

Joe Skuba, Florida – a good 100-meter freestyle swimmer and a good guy. An aerobic-based programme suited Skuba. In two years, his personal best improved by 3.19 seconds (5.9%) from 54.14 to 50.95. When I left Florida, Skuba shifted to a popular sprint-based team and did not improve his 100 time. In three years on the sprint team even his 50-meter time only improved by 0.27 seconds (1.2%) from 23.38 to 23.11 The message is: Choose a programme that suits you, not one that the in-crowd says is the place to be.

CHAPTER 14

TOO MUCH SPEED TRAINING

This chapter is not a tirade against speed training. I have already said that speed training should form 40% and anaerobic training 20% of a season's training. So, in one form or another, fast-paced swimming occupies a majority: 60% of a season's training. My concern is programmes that go well beyond 60%; programmes that reduce or even miss out altogether the aerobic period of training. I have mentioned the national coach in Saudi Arabia. Only 4% of his main sets had an aerobic purpose; 96% of his training time was spent on anaerobic or speed sessions. And that is a poorly balanced programme likely to cause early career dropout.

The Saudi Arabian government spends millions of Riyal sending swimmers all over the world in the hope that exposing them to international competition will lift the standard of the nation's swimming. But it is wasted money when the swimmers come home and swim in a 96% speed only programme.

The problem is not unique to Saudi Arabia. There are plenty of programmes like that around the world. They lack balance. There are several facts that disguise the dangers of too much speed training, summarized in the next table.

Dangers Disguised by Excessive Speed Training

1. Short-term results are spectacular and lead to misplaced confidence of success.
2. Results in young swimmers are spectacular but also lead to misplaced confidence of success.
3. Dangers often do not appear until it is too late for remedial measures to work.
4. Speed training matches many stereotypes. It looks right. It seems more like "real" training.
5. It has many academic supporters and fitness slogan backers.
6. Coaches love the commercial benefit of pushing the concept of "half the work for twice the gain".

Without question, the high priest of speed training is the American coach, Dave Salo. He has provided the theoretical basis and the practical example of speed training for hundreds of coaches worldwide to follow. Despite his influential arguments in support of intense speed training, remember that if it sounds too good to be true, it probably is.

In 1993, Salo published *SprintSalo*. In the book, he acknowledged that his views on speed swimming were founded on questioning the validity of swimming long aerobic distances for races that often lasted less than a minute. Wouldn't it be better, he argued, for the speed, intensity and distance of a swimmer's training to closely mirror the swimmer's race event? Training, he said, should be a "competitive experience". A well-designed 3000-meter session was a far more effective way to achieve good competitive results than swimming 8000 meters at a medium pace. Further, he argued, swimmers in his short sprint-based programme were more willing to work harder and "accept their exhaustion".

Experiencing the stress of fast swimming, Salo said, best enhances anaerobic capacity and improves the ability to buffer lactic acid generated in the working muscles. To be at all effective, training "must involve intense race pace swims."

While Salo might be the high priest of sprint training, he is not short of loyal disciples. There are a variety of sources supporting the idea of training less for more from many with a background that lends credibility to their claims. But, another word of caution, there are no shortcuts to the top.

I think we can agree that many claims in support of speed training sound attractive. As Salo says in his book, *SprintSalo*, "If you're going to play the piano… don't practice the tuba!" According to Salo, interval training is the answer. Lie in bed for an extra hour and get a better result in the pool. That must be good. And it is good. Remember that the balanced programme being proposed here is 60% of just the sort of training Salo is promoting. It is the dangers and limitations, especially to young swimmers, of 90 to 100% high-intensity programmes that are of concern.

Simply looking at a list of the 20 Olympians coached by Salo and assuming the type of training he promotes will take an aspiring pre-teen to Olympic success is not the full story. Most of Salo's 20 Olympians came to him after being grounded in aerobic-based programmes.

Rebecca Soni was a high school graduate before swimming with Salo; Jessica Hardy came from Teri McKeever. Aaron Peirsol swam with Eddie Reese. Lenny Krayzelburg trained with Mark Schubert. Oussama Mellouli and Katinka Hosszu were both raised and received their early swim training half a world away from Salo in Southern California.

Of course, swimmers raised in a sound aerobic programme are going to respond well to the high-intensity training promoted by Salo. In their early club programmes, these swimmers had already built a firm aerobic base; they were aerobically well conditioned and receptive to the demands of high-intensity anaerobic training. For as long as their early aerobic training held up, mature swimmers benefit from Salo's intense speed programme. The success of these Olympic swimmers has no relevance to the suitability of Salo's methods throughout a swimmer's career.

Initially, even young, immature swimmers are also going to respond well to the training used by Salo. High-intensity anaerobic training is the very best way to exploit their natural talent. Problems only appear when natural talent reaches its limit and the swimmers have matured. Then, because no aerobic base has been put in place, there is nothing left to build on, and another swimming career wanes and dies. By the time the problem is diagnosed it is already too late.

It is serious. Just like the negative effects of too much racing and too much speed training can be similarly dangerous for, of course, the same reasons. The physiological damage caused by excessive racing is identical to the damage done by excessive and constant Salo-type training.

Salo himself describes this as follows:

> *"Under circumstances of intense racing many things are happening in the swimmer's body. For this reason it is important that the body experience this type of stress in order that appropriate adaptations can occur. Training to enhance the anaerobic capacity, therefore, must involve intense race pace swims."*

What Salo is saying is that every training session should replicate the physical stress of competition; a race every day.

Therefore, if you are a parent and you notice your child coming out of the pool most days with a story about how fast and hard their training was today, don't congratulate yourself on finding the perfect coach. If sprints are their daily diet, if their coach is a Salo disciple, it might be time to look for another coach. What their current coach is doing is probably dangerous. Short-term performance gains disguise a problem in the making. Improved times provide confidence that all is well when in fact the seeds of failure are being nurtured.

ARTHUR LYDIARD'S THOUGHTS ON SPEED TRAINING

"I have a saying: 'train, don't strain.' The Americans have the saying: 'no pain, no gain' and that's why they have no distance running champions. They get down to the track with a stopwatch and flog their guts out, thinking that it'll make them a champion, but they'll never make a champion that way."

"Know your limits and stay within them. Do what you think you can cope with."

"If you are not enjoying training, stop all anaerobic training. Go out for a long jog, so slow that the old ladies with shopping baskets go past you. Do that until you start to enjoy it!"

It is worthwhile stressing again that the training proposed here does not exclude Salo-type training. 60% of a balanced programme is very similar to Salo's programme. In fact, asked the question, which section of a balanced programme is the most important, without hesitation I would select the speed period. That is the time to get ready to race.

All the training tools recommended by Salo have a place in a balanced programme: pulse plots, time trials, descending sets, ascending sets, broken sets, short intervals, hard effort long intervals and many more. The intent here is simply to advise balance and caution.

In the speed work period of training, the Salo test is a very useful tool for measuring training performance. More importantly it can act as an early indicator of training overload. Recognizing when training and competition are leading to excessive stress is vital to preventing overtraining and early dropout. The Salo test identifies symptoms of overtraining. When all is going well, the pulse plot reference line will shift in a curve to the right. When things are not going well, when overtraining may be a problem, there will be a leftward shift in the pulse plot reference line.

What the pulse plot test is saying is that overtrained swimmers will have an increased heart rate at slower speeds and their recovery will take longer. When this trend is observed, overtraining is very near. Remedial steps need to be taken. Since over training Toni Jeffs prior to the Barcelona Olympic Games I have used the Salo PulsePlot and have identified and corrected cases of overtraining before they became serious. In the speed work period I have swimmers perform the pulse plot set every three weeks. That assessment has been an invaluable tool in enabling me to maintain a high-performance programme without overtraining swimmers – in other words, to stay fresh and sharp.

At the most, the combined anaerobic and speed training periods should last no more than 14 weeks in a six-month season (28 weeks in a year). Swimmers, young and old, cannot maintain the physical demands of racing and sprinting for longer than that. They need time to recharge the batteries. Failure to do so will exponentially increase swimmer's chances of injury or send them to surf lifesaving, water polo or, even more likely, into early retirement.

SALO'S PULSEPLOT

The PulsePlot procedure is not a difficult set to perform. PulsePlot is based on two concepts. First, an increase in the heart rate accompanies an increase in swimming intensity. Second, the better conditioned swimmer will recover more quickly following a swim. The set involves swimming eight 100s at a 4:30 interval. The first four 100s have a descending finish time, (70%, 80%, 90% and 100% effort), and then the last four 100s have an ascending finish time, (100%, 90%, 80% and 70% effort). Following each swim the swimmer takes a :10 second heart rate count immediately after finishing, :30 seconds after finishing and then :60 seconds after finishing. The times and the cumulative heart rates should then be plotted and a line drawn through them. The line or PulsePlot describes the effect of swimming intensity on cardiovascular condition. By repeating this set periodically the swimmer and the coach can better monitor the training.*

---

* From SprintSalo by David C. Salo, PhD. (1993) Sports Support Syndicate, Inc, p. 30.

Before I began coaching Eyad Masoud, he was doing 15 kilometers a week of sprint training. He now does a balanced programme of 60 kilometers a week and has improved his racing times by 5% in 10 months.

CHAPTER 15

LACK OF PERIODIZATION

Calculating and incorporating the correct amount of rest into a swimmer's training is just as important as the swimming content. There are numerous rest periods to consider: periods of weeks between seasons, of days between hard sets, of hours between sessions and of seconds between set intervals. Important rules apply to these rest periods. Failure to observe correct rest procedures will have a negative effect on performance. Too much rest and swimmers will not improve. Too little rest and stress will accumulate, and swimmers will exhibit symptoms of overtraining. Both problems can lead to early dropout from the sport.

Remember – swimmers get fit while they rest, not while they train. Progress is made by stressing the body and allowing it to adapt and recover. Progressive stress followed by time for the body to adapt to that stress is how training works. As the body recovers during rest periods, it adapts and gets stronger. An athlete who simply piles stress upon stress without rest is not going to improve.

Let's look at the factors that are important in calculating the correct amount of rest.

SEASON AND PERIOD HOLIDAYS

A balanced programme includes three training periods: aerobic training for 10 weeks, anaerobic for 4 weeks and speed for 10 weeks. In addition, I programme three "holiday" weeks, making a full season total of 27 weeks.

The first "holiday" week I call a "Get Back In" week at the beginning of each season. The swimmer is about to undertake 10 weeks of long aerobic training. It has been 17 weeks since the swimmer last swam this sort of programme and these distances. Crashing straight into long aerobic distances is asking for trouble. For all the thousands of miles and hundreds of races run by Alison, she only ever had one injury. That was in a season where she was running well and went straight into the aerobic build-up for a new season, running 100 miles a week. Actually, she didn't run 100 miles. After two days of the first week, she had so badly damaged her Achilles tendon that she needed three weeks of treatment before she could run again.

Since then I have included a "Get Back In" week and have never had an athlete suffer a similar early season injury. Normally I programme about 40% of the planned build-up weekly mileage. Swimmers planning on training 100 kilometers a week in the build-up would swim 40 kilometers in the "Get Back In" week. Swimmers planning very high mileages of 120 kilometers a week or more during the build-up would be wise to consider reaching that total by including two "Get Back In" weeks.

Because this week is a period of adjustment, I do not include any fast swimming. The bulk of the training should be some long swims of 1,500 or 2,000 meters, a set of 50x100 on 1.30 and similar easy aerobic swimming. Longer, steady kick and pull sets should be introduced. The adaption process is aided by including all four strokes.

The remaining two holiday weeks are programmed in two periods. The first holiday, of one week, is included at the end of the 10-week aerobic build-up and before the four weeks of anaerobic training. Swimmers are fit but tired from long conditioning swims. Before getting into the much faster stress of anaerobic swimming, it is beneficial to allow a week to recover. A holiday week at this stage is simply a means of avoiding the coaching sin of piling stress upon stress with no time to recover.

The final holiday week is allocated to a break at the end of the racing season and before beginning the next season's build-up. There are two reasons for this holiday. First is the need to recover from a long, 10-week racing season. Swimmers have just completed their pinnacle competition and physically and psychologically are ready for a rest. Second, career people in every activity have an annual holiday. Swimmers should observe the same discipline.

Holiday weeks should include some swimming. Staying away from the pool completely can make it difficult to get started again. For mature swimmers, 4 or 5 kilometers of easy swimming done in two sessions is all that is necessary to maintain a feel of the water. Junior swimmers should swim 2 kilometers each holiday week in two sessions.

The next table shows a full six-month season plan, highlighting the "Get Back In" and the holiday weeks.

NAME OF PERIOD	NUMBER OF WEEKS
Get Back In	1
Build-up aerobic	10
Holiday	1
Anaerobic	4
Speed	10
Holiday	1
Total	27

THE HARD DAY, EASY DAY RULE

At every stage of training it is important to observe the "hard day, easy day" rule. In the aerobic build-up period, the total distance and time spent in the water results in the planned physiological changes. In these weeks, therefore, hard training actually means long training. The following table shows a training plan for a typical build-up week. Three very long days are interspersed with four recovery days. Younger swimmers should follow the same pattern.

In the anaerobic period, the "hard day, easy day" rule is no longer related to the distance being swum. At this stage, the quality and difficulty of the weekly anaerobic sets become the determining factors. Since these sets are highly stressful, they should never be done more than three days a week. Swimmers will lose the benefit of the training if they do more than that. They will be prone to injury and will not have enough time for rest and repair. The table shows the pattern used for a mature swimmer. Junior swimmers will swim less distance and should only swim the hard anaerobic sets twice a week.

DAY	BUILD-UP AEROBIC TRAINING DIFFICULTY	ANAEROBIC TRAINING DIFFICULTY
Monday	Recovery	Recovery
Tuesday	Long	Hard anaerobic
Wednesday	Recovery	Recovery
Thursday	Long	Hard anaerobic
Friday	Recovery	Recovery
Saturday	Long	Hard anaerobic
Sunday	Recovery	Recovery

The "hard day, easy day" rule changes in the speed section of training. At this stage, none of the training should be as physically stressful as in the aerobic and anaerobic periods. As we have already discussed, the key words in this period are "fresh and sharp". I set aside each morning swim and two of the afternoon swims as aerobic recovery sessions and the remaining five afternoon sessions provide the sprint, time trial, fartlek and review sessions swum in this period.

REST BETWEEN INTERVALS

The length of rest between repetitions in a training set depends on the stage of training. Different length rests apply depending on whether the training purpose is aerobic, anaerobic or speed. What is certain is that the length of rest is important; it cannot be left to chance.

In the aerobic period, the main training sets are swum at close to aerobic threshold pace. In other words, at a pace where the oxygen from breathing is still just sufficient to supply the energy required. The physiological changes important to the swimmer are produced by continuous, steady effort over a long period. At aerobic swimming speed, rest is not required. In fact, rest can defeat the aerobic purpose because it interrupts the continuous and steady quality of aerobic training. Research scientists in Finland who studied the effect of different periods of rest established that rests of 15 seconds or less had little or no recovery benefit. Therefore, physiologically 100x100 done with 15 seconds of rest between each 100 is physiologically the same as a 10-kilometer straight swim. The benefit of the rest is primarily psychological. For this reason, in the aerobic period, to preserve the aerobic purpose, it is important for rests to be short, preferably less than 15 seconds and never more than 30 seconds.

In the anaerobic period, the speed of the main training sets increases. Therefore, the planned rest now has an important recovery purpose. The same Finnish scientists who determined the 15-second aerobic rest discovered that optimum anaerobic results are achieved when the activity continues for 30 minutes. Therefore, the trick in achieving the best anaerobic improvement is to plan the swimmer's speed and rest in order that the session is swum at the maximum, consistent speed possible while still lasting 30 minutes. But what must not happen is for the rest to be so long that the swimmer recovers completely between swims.

The best way to determine the rest is to monitor the swimmer's heart rate. During the swim, the swimmer's heart rate is raised into the anaerobic range of around 200 bpm. The swimmer then monitors his or her 10-second heart rate and when it returns to 130 bpm swims the next repetition. The rest is controlled by the swimmer's recovery. If the rate does not recover in two minutes, the swimmer should stop. The purpose of the set has been achieved. If the heart rate does recover, the set continues until completion.

An individual heart rate recovery protocol is best but, in a squad situation, is not always practical. When a team is swimming an anaerobic set, it is usually necessary to use a pace clock. Achieving the best rest varies depending on the length of each repetition. For short repetitions of 50 or 100 meters I normally set between 30-second and 1-minute rests. For longer 400-metrt repetitions, I normally allow between 1:30 and 2:00 minutes of rest. The timed rest should replicate, as far as possible, the rest that would apply if swimmers were able to use their heart rate recovery.

There is no harm in allowing a longer rest toward the end of a set. This promotes the effectiveness of the set by allowing swimmers to go further into an anaerobic condition and does reflect what happens if the swimmers were basing their recovery on heart rate.

In the speed period of training, freshness and sharpness are paramount. Therefore, rest assumes even more importance. In most instances, a full recovery is necessary to ensure a series of fast efforts. Of course, the length of rest will depend on the distance of each repetition. Even for a short effort of 50 meters, sufficient recovery requires a minimum of 1 minute, 30 seconds. Longer swims need up to five or six minutes between efforts. To many this may seem like far too much rest. The correct training protocols, however, cannot be rushed. Nature takes time to adjust the accumulation of metabolic by-products (lactic acid, for example). Replenishment of phosphagen can take two or three minutes, depending on the length of the high-intensity interval. Good training in the speed period demands compliance with the biological processes involved in recovery.

A common theme repeated many times is the danger to both junior and senior swimmers of overtraining. "Harder must be better" is an easy mistake made in swim teams all over the world. I have coached swimmers who have sneaked off to the pool for another training session rather than observe a programmed rest. (I am not including the aforementioned Abigail in this category, as she cleared her extra-long training swim with me first!) On the whole, however, this is wrong. In the speed period, especially, fewer repetitions and more rest might reduce the effort required over the full session. However, the peak power obtained in the workout and the frequency of reaching peak power will be higher. And that is good.

All this is summarised in the following table.

TYPE OF TRAINING PERIOD	LENGTH OF REST
Aerobic training period	Less than 30 seconds
Anaerobic training period	Between 0.30 seconds and 1.30
Speed training period	Longer than 1.30 and up to 6.00 minutes

Finally, there is the question of what should be done during the rest intervals? What is the best form of recovery? The answer is light active exercise. After a hard swim of 400 meters, an easy swim of 50 or 100 meters to recover helps maintain good blood flow and therefore aids the recovery process. Sedentary rest is fine for short efforts that mainly use the oxidative system and therefore do not produce much lactic acid.

All this talk about the importance of rest does not change the programme's recommendation of seven days a week training for senior swimmers. Is this a contradiction? Not at all. In every training period, the swimming recommended for Sunday is a comparatively shorter and easier aerobic swim. As has been discussed, easy active rest is the very best form of recovery. The seven-day programme does not damage recovery; it aids the recovery process.

Lydiard put it best when he growled, "If you miss one day a week, that's 52 days a year, that's a month and a half of training missed." Done properly it's a month and a half of good, active recovery.

Florida team members just finished Saturday's 100x100 on 1.30 – Skuba, Tori, Andrew and me. Tori was a triathlete who swam with our team. Skuba was Florida 100 freestyle champion and Andrew was 100 freestyle Florida State High School Champion.

CHAPTER 16

DON'T TIME EVERYTHING

In one of my favourite Arthur Lydiard quotes, he describes the unstructured coaching style likely to yield the best results:

• How far? To the next tree.

• How fast? Your best effort.

• How many? Until you get tired.

And Lydiard was as good as his word. He told me he had done a successful training session with Dick Taylor, the 1974 Commonwealth Games 10,000-meter champion, that involved sprinting along the fairways of a Christchurch golf course. Arthur did not measure the distance or count the number of repetitions, and they were certainly not timed. What mattered, Lydiard explained, was the effect the training was having, and Taylor knew what that should be better than anyone.

Several years ago, I took Lydiard to the finals of the Auckland Swimming Championships. When we arrived, the pre-meet warm-up was in full swing. Lydiard said to me, "What are they doing?" I looked around and could not see anything unusual and so asked, "What do you mean?"

"All those coaches with all those stopwatches – what are they doing?"

And then it dawned on me. Arthur had never seen the coaching ritual that goes on before the beginning of your average swim meet.

One well-known coach is in a performance master class when it comes to his pre-race warm-up display. He dashes along the pool, two stopwatches at the ready. And if a timed swim – this is somewhat redundant; they are all timed swims – happens to end in the middle of the pool, he raises an arm with circled fingers providing theodolite accuracy. The swimmer is then told his time to the hundredth of a second.

This coach is admired by many impressed by his effort, unaware that all that energy and all those times are most likely in the process of ending a swimmer's fledgling career. And this guy, while he might be exceptional, is certainly not alone.

A dozen coaches work hard to emulate the same enthusiasm. Being a master coach requires two triple display Seiko S141 100 memory stopwatches. Most coaches wear them as a formal livery collar, but a few casual sorts have the cords hanging carelessly from their pockets. I don't know how they manage two watches. I have difficulty getting one right.

A cardinal Lydiard rule is avoid loading swimmers with race tactics and information on the day of a race. On race day, swimmers should be free to collect their own thoughts and rehearse their strategy. A good coach's input should have been communicated well before race day and well before the warm-up for the event.

But back to my hyperactive coach: I've heard him correcting strokes and race pace decisions in the warm-up before a national championship. Changing a swimmer's stroke one hour before an event makes no sense at all. It simply means the tuition that should have taken place in the training pool was neglected. Air New Zealand does not wait until their Boeing is taxiing for take-off to check whether the pilot knows how to fly.

Overuse of a stopwatch in training can also cause stress and early career dropout. With junior swimmers I seldom use a stopwatch – certainly almost never in the aerobic and anaerobic periods of training. In the speed period, I do time the time trials. On these occasions, I make the event as exciting as possible – a "time opportunity" rather than a "time trial". Always I compare the result with the junior swimmer's previous time trial best rather than as a race against others. Done properly, junior swimmers look forward to being timed.

Many senior swimmers have joined my team and clearly fear the appearance of a stopwatch. Their attitude is the result of coaches misusing a stopwatch earlier in their careers. No one should be fearful of being timed. Used well, a stopwatch is an opportunity to excel. Used badly, it becomes a thing of stress and anxiety.

With senior swimmers in the aerobic and anaerobic periods, never time the easy recovery sessions. That would be a contradiction. In both periods of training, I might time the Tuesday, Thursday and Saturday main sets, but even that is not compulsory. The training can be just as effective timed or untimed – remember Dick Taylor. In these periods of training, I ask the swimmer whether they want the main sets timed. If they say yes, I time them. If they say no, they would prefer to focus on applying the correct effort without the pressure of having the swim timed, then I do not time the swims. This seems to work. Swimmers enjoy controlling this feature of their training.

Obviously in the speed period of training, a stopwatch gets more use. Time trials certainly need to be timed. Split times are a valuable aid in detecting speed or fitness problems. Early speed followed by slower lap times suggests a fitness problem that should be addressed by a firm session of anaerobic swims. Even splits at a speed slower than the expected race pace suggest some additional speed training is needed. Slow splits at the start followed by a fast finish can either be a fitness problem or just bad pace judgement. Split times in these swims are an essential aid in the evaluation and correction process.

As swimmers work toward full racing speed, sprint sets should also be timed. But even in this period it is important to stress on swimmers that the time they swim is only one measure of performance. The number of strokes, their stroke rhythm, correct underwater work during the start and turn and good technique are things the swimmer can control. During a time trial, these things are more important than the final time on a stopwatch.

Equally important to overactive coaches is the accessory of a whistle. I have never used one. The comparison with New Zealand sheep dog trials makes me uncomfortable. For a meet referee a whistle is fine, but not for a coach. Human beings communicate best using words, not a whistle.

Don't be like a coach who worked for me at a club in Wellington, New Zealand. When I arrived at the club, I asked him into my office to discuss his training policy and his plans to progress the team. He told me that he had developed a revolutionary new approach to world class swimming. It was simple. All he needed to do, he said, was calculate the time gap between where the swimmer was now and the time required to be world class. He then divided that by the number of two-week periods in four years – 104. Then he had the swimmer sprint short timed sets every day and at the end of each two weeks swim a time trial. He said that he expected the planned small improvement. Do that 104 times and in four years the club would have a world class swimmer. For example, a modest female 1:05 100-meter swimmer, he explained, would be swimming a 0:53 second 100 meters with just a 0.1 second improvement in each of the 104 time trials.

"What happens," I asked, "if the swimmer misses the improvement?" Well, he said, he would increase the sprinting volume for two weeks and the planned improvements would come back into line. After several weeks of trying to convince him a more orthodox approach of aerobic, anaerobic and speed might be better, I had to ask him to leave. He is still coaching. I have not heard of any female 0:53 second 100-meter swimmers coming from his new club.

In summary, a stopwatch is a harsh judge of a swimmer's performance. It cannot take into account how swimmers feel or what else is going on in their lives. No one enjoys being judged to the hundredth of a second every day, twice a day. If you want to see your swimmers enjoy the sport and soar to its highest levels, use a stopwatch with caution.

How it all begins: Boy's 50 freestyle waiting to start in Jeddah, Saudi Arabia

CHAPTER 17

AVOID MONOTONOUS TRAINING

Like most things, all work and no play can quickly lead to boredom and burnout. Certainly, training well is more difficult when day after day similar sets are written on the coach's whiteboard.

Just about every swimmer who decides to retire at some stage mentions the monotony of constantly looking at a black line on the bottom of the pool. I knew one good swimmer who claimed she had counted the number of small tiles in her 50-meter lane. Many swimmers can accurately identify pools from all over the world, but especially those in which they trained the most many years later from photos of the pools' floors.

On the same subject, I recently received a text from Eyad Masoud, one of my swimmers in Saudi Arabia. This is what he said: "I did my training today and it was fun, not the 3K kicking, that was a patience test, but I passed. I counted the joints of the ceiling stiffeners (196) and 18 vertical rods and 23 horizontal rods."

Eyad Masoud, counting "196 ceiling stiffeners" partway through his 3,000 kick

Having said that fun should be injected into swim practice, it is not easy to transform daily swim training into a gala event. Successful swimming requires that certain sets must be swum. Seldom is that easy or fun. Good coaches seem to be able to generate interest in two ways. Some use the power of their personality to inspire and lead. Others are skilled enough to get the hard work done and at the same time incorporate games and fun into their training.

Olympic coach Mark Schubert and my old coach from Gisborne in New Zealand, Beth Meade, are examples of personality coaches. I could not wait to get back to training to find out what impossible task Beth was going to demand next. We were made to swim across Gisborne harbour on a freezing day in the middle of winter. We did a week-long school holiday training camp at a hot springs pool where the water temperature was far hotter than a bath at home. We received a tap on the shoulders from Beth's trusty length of hose used to remind us that more effort was required. We smiled as Beth pushed and shoved, asked and demanded more effort. And did it work? Most certainly – our club had the largest membership in the country. We won the team provincial championship every year and one year by more points than all the other clubs together. But, best of all, Beth instilled a love of swimming that has lasted a lifetime.

Two coaches stand out as masters of the art of incorporating games and fun into the serious business of swim training. Johnathan Winter, currently the head coach at the Raumati Club in Wellington, New Zealand, and Abigail Frink, an assistant coach who worked for me at West Auckland Aquatics in Auckland, New Zealand. Here are some of the odd things I've seen them do and others that have been suggested to me. Some of them I have even tried.

OPEN WATER PRACTICE
This suggestion was first made by track coach Arthur Lydiard. He compared the freedom experienced by his athletes training through the Waitakere Ranges with the confined world of competitive swimming. "Why not," he asked, "let your swimmers do some of their build-up aerobic training in a lake?" I've experimented with the idea for several years by encouraging swimmers to enter 10-kilometer open water swims. Purists would be horrified at a 50-meter specialist swimming 10 kilometers around Lake Taupo. But as an event to inspire interest and challenge, it has been stunningly successful. The 50-meter types walk around for months telling anyone who will listen about the day they swam around Lake Taupo.

STROKE ANALYSIS
The danger of too much stroke correction is "paralysis by analysis". I know of an ex-national coach who is a machine gun of stroke advice. There is no way any swimmer could possibly keep up with his stream of instructions. However, applied sensibly, providing some stroke correction is a valuable way to improve swimmer's technique and take their minds off the monotony of repetitive lengths of swimming.

AUDIO
An innovation that does work is an Mp3 player. Listening to music is a great training aid. I first read about the idea in an article about the master French coach, Fabrice Pellerin. Depending on the set being swum he went as far as to select the music his swimmers listened to – some aggressive Mozart for a speed set, some Handel for a gentle warm-up and the playful exuberance of Vivaldi to get through a hard anaerobic set. I've never gone as far as selecting the music but have had many swimmers use an Mp3 player. Olympic Gold

medallist, Rhi Jeffrey, swore by the idea, and it didn't seem to do her any harm. One good swimmer from a strict Christian family even went as far as to bring a waterproof plastic bible to training. She read away happily during long aerobic kick sets. Acts 27:43 seemed appropriate: "those who could swim should jump overboard first and get to land."

DRILLS AND COUNTING

Using drills and asking swimmers to count their strokes are important training aids. They have the added benefit of keeping swimmers' minds occupied. We have discussed the 20 drills I use as a regular part of training. Counting strokes is also important for swimmers wanting to improve their performance. It is not something that works as a distraction for long. After a short time of counting strokes, swimmers just know, without counting, how many strokes each length has taken.

ALL FOUR STROKES

There are significant technique benefits that accrue as a result of including all four strokes in a training programme. Australian Swimming has long recommended that medley training is the foundation of all young swimmers' early development. It is a rule with a lot of merit. The wider muscle movement, different feel of the water and mixed coordination required by practicing all four strokes are important skill developments. The variety also eases the monotony of a hundred identical laps. As preferences emerge, stroke and distance specialization can occur later.

SENIOR SWIMMERS' WORKOUTS

Most senior swimmers have an intimate understanding of the meaning of aerobic, anaerobic and speed training. They appreciate fully the difference between a recovery and a work session. With this in mind, I have frequently asked swimmers to prepare their own training workout. Of course, I check to make sure the required training purpose is being achieved. When I have made changes, it has usually been to soften a too harsh training set. These guys can be tough. Even with young swimmers it is fun to ask, "What would you like to do today?" Almost always you get sensible and constructive replies. "Relays" is, of course, the most frequent answer.

GET THE FEDERATION TO DO SOMETHING

Different It is not surprising that swimmers making their ninth or tenth visit to the local state championships find it difficult to generate the enthusiasm they once had. Over time even the attraction of a national championship can begin to wane – same competitors same officials and often the same pool. In an effort to relieve some of the monotony I have taken swimmers to overseas events as much as possible. However, there is more federations could do to brighten up the annual schedule. For example, in Saudi Arabia, they have a National Fins Championship. They swim butterfly, backstroke and freestyle events up to 200 meters. They have national records and award national championship certificates. It is a fun event, something different. FINA is trying to do a similar thing with mixed relays being introduced to world events. It is difficult for swimming to match the beach race, surf board, rescue boat and swim rescue variety of surf competition. But there is a lot more swimming could do.

Loai, Eyad and Mohamed – Individual Fins Championship winners from our team

FINALLY – BE A KID AGAIN

I'm not good at this, but I have seen Jonathan and Abigail introduce fun games into their daily practice. Jonathan frequently uses water polo and relays. I saw his squad doing 50-meter intervals broken with a dive to the bottom of the pool halfway down the length. I can hear Lydiard growling already that he had never seen that event at an Olympic Games. But Jonathan's squad seemed be enjoying the set. Certainly, he has a reputation for providing the happiest and some of the most successful programmes in New Zealand swimming. Abigail was great at inventing games for young swimmers. I've seen her have pool candy scrambles, coach face painting, silly stroke races and as, a special treat, well-behaved swimmers were occasionally allowed to push their fully clothed coach into the pool. Abigail was brilliant at balancing the difficult mix of fun and work.

So there are some ideas. Making an activity that takes place between two walls 25 meters apart fun is not easy, especially when the exact distance of every length is bliss to a fanatic with a stopwatch. But make an effort at providing variety and interest. You will be rewarded by swimmers enjoying swimming more and staying in the sport longer.

CHAPTER 18

SOME SUNDRY ITEMS

There are several minor issues that, if handled properly, can make a swimmer's journey easier and will help avoid early career dropout.

TEACH SKILLS EARLY

Swimmers often join a competitive team with poorly taught basic skills. Correct basics are not complicated. They should be taught early.

The best example in swimming is breaststroke kick. The narrow kick that is now standard in the swimming world was first used in the late 1960s. That was 50 years ago. Yet dozens of young swimmers graduate from swim schools where they still teach the old-fashioned circular "frog" kick. The "whip" kick is just as easy to learn, so why swim schools persist with the old kick is beyond reason. What is annoying for the coach and the swimmer is the need to stop the old kick and reteach the new skill.

Swimming New Zealand published an excellent learn to swim manual called "Kiwi Swim Safe". Their description of the breaststroke kick says, "Aim for knees not   separating more than shoulder width. Feel pressure on feet especially the instep." So the national federation have it right. Swim schools just need to follow.

While this example is the most common, there are other recurrent cases of poor learn to swim tuition that make life for the junior swimmer more difficult. The following table gives some examples.

LEARN TO SWIM MISTAKE	REASON
Never swim with straight arms.	Why not? Janet Evans did and Florent Manaudou does, and both of them have won Olympic championships swimming with straight arms. It is not a mistake
Don't bend your knees in the freestyle kick.	Why not? Every Olympic swimmer flexes their knees during the freestyle kick. It is impossible to generate leg speed with straight legs.
One-arm freestyle is a good drill.	No, it is not. It causes the swimmer to drop the wrong shoulder.
The Otter drill is wasted lesson time.	It is actually one of the best drills. The swimmer duck dives to the bottom, then comes to the surface, rolls over on his back, rolls back again and goes into the next duck dive. For water skills, Otter is as good as they get. I learned this drill from the East German national coach, Mike Regner. He used it on swimmers on the East German national team and said it had contributed greatly to their feel for smooth movement through the water. He said, "If you want someone to swim like a fish, they have to feel like a fish."
Always stretch before a lesson.	No, never stretch a cold muscle. Warm up first and then stretch. This rule is broken by teams around the world and is the cause of injury problems. Stroke drills are swimming specific and are the best method of stretching.
Distance per stroke and stroke rhythm only need to be taught to senior swimmers.	The importance of increasing the size of a swimmer's stroke, counting strokes and holding a set rhythm are skills that should be taught as part of the learn to swim curriculum.
The freestyle pull should begin thumb first and follow an S-shape pattern.	No, fingers first into the catch and then a straight pull. Because of the roll of shoulders and hips, the hand does follow a shallow S shape but feels straight to the swimmer. Exaggerated S-shaped pulls are a thing of the past.
Always teach a strict breathing pattern.	No, nothing stops you faster than a lack of air. We have been through the era of trying to get swimmers to swim as far as possible without breathing. In all events longer than 50 meters, breath frequently to either side.

KEEP IT SIMPLE

Sticking to the basics usually means keeping it simple. If it looks odd, it is probably wrong. Jack-knife dives, flicking wrists and strange breathing patterns are affectations with no purpose. You hardly notice good swimmers. Everything they do is the simple things done well.

The best example was provided by New Zealand's most successful swimming coach, Duncan Laing. One evening he was asked to stand in and coach an under-12 rugby team. The normal coach said he had been doing lineout practice and asked Laing to revise the lesson.

Laing asked the team to show him what they had learned. The boy throwing the ball into the lineout called an impressive list of numbers and threw the ball. No one could catch it, so Duncan abandoned the sophisticated lineout drills and did an hour of catching practice. In sport, simple does not mean wrong.

Master coaches like Duncan Laing, Mark Schubert, Arthur Lydiard and Arch Jelley make and keep it all so simple. They are brilliant at cutting through the confusion. For Lydiard, winning the Olympics was a matter of doing this, this and this and winning the race – simple really. I remember Jelley being asked by an Auckland administrator, known for making simple things complicated, how he would spend $2 million to improve swimming. Jelley thought for a minute and said, "That's a lot of money." I could tell that the administrator left wondering how someone like Jelley ended up coaching so many champion runners. Sad thing was the administrator had just found out but never understood the message.

The better the coach, the easier swimming seems to be. I've had discussions with coaches about swimming matters and have left not understanding a word they have said. One national coach was incredible. I asked him what he thought was a good weekly mileage for a senior international swimmer. He talked for 20 minutes, and I still don't know the answer. Poor coaches camouflage their shortcomings in a forest of complexity. If you can't understand your coach, if you leave feeling the coach must be really clever to understand a subject as complex as swimming, get another coach.

POOR TEENAGE DIET

Most of us accept that poor eating habits combined with strenuous exercise are likely to lead to problems that could end a promising swimming career. But what is a good diet? How should an athlete eat to fuel the effort of swim training?

Well, what is not right are some of the crazy things done by coaches to reduce athlete's body weight, especially comments aimed at female swimmers. Calling athletes, male or female, fat and pigs is no way to behave. All that stuff is outright abuse and has no place in sport or in life. In fact, that behaviour is likely to be responsible for serious eating disorders and early retirement.

During gym training, I frequently get swimmers to weigh themselves. I explain that I want to check that they are not losing too much weight. Weight loss can indicate overtraining. Using that as the reason avoids swimmers getting paranoid about their diet and fearful of recording their weight.

I have always promoted the Stanford diet. It got its name after being used for many years by the successful Stanford University swim team. The diet is described in the book *Enter the Zone* by Barry Sears.

The Stanford diet promotes an intake ratio of 35% protein, 35% carbohydrate and 30% fat. Those ratios are lower in carbohydrate and higher in fat that most nutritionists recommend. The reason, of course, is that fat is a valuable fuel source for athletes swimming 14 kilometers a day, six or seven days a week. In reality, what that means is the diet recommends eating a normal balance of foods. Don't cut out foods traditionally labelled fatty. Have peanut butter sandwiches for lunch and a meat, potatoes and vegetable dinner. The higher fat intake is needed and will be well used by the end of the night's workout. The message then is a balanced diet.

If you are female and have a coach who insults your body weight, find another coach.

FAILURE TO WARM UP AND COOL DOWN

Good training requires swimmers to warm up before and cool down after hard physical exercise. Failure to do either properly can quickly lead to unnecessary injury and early retirement. There is no way I am advocating the demanding training sessions some coaches push their swimmers through prior to a big event. These coaches appear to enjoy looking tough by handing out the harshest warm-up. One very good swimmer told me her coach had asked her to do a set of 16x200 prior to the heats of the European Championships. What that was supposed to prove is anyone's guess.

Not warming up properly can be a cause of early dropout. Crazy warm-ups like 16x200 will achieve the same result except more quickly. For a senior swimmer, I have found between 1,500 and 2,000 meters of mixed swimming to be about right. For juniors, between 500 and 1000 meters is plenty.

DRYLAND WEIGHT TRAINING

The weight training programme I recommend has been described in detail in my first book, *Swim to the Top*. Some caution is, however, required. The programme is very specific to swimming. The range of 24 exercises, the recommended weights and the number of repetitions are tailored to aid swimming performance by providing power not achievable in the pool. But be careful, I have found that while female swimmers seem happy to follow the programme, you can't trust the males. Turn your back for five minutes and guys, especially in Saudi Arabia, are spending their time beating their mates in the three "male ego" exercises: squats, biceps curls and bench presses. Ironically, those three are also the exercises least useful to swimming. I remind the guys that their purpose in the gym is to improve their swimming, not to create Mr. Universe.

Eyad Masoud in Saudi Arabia does his morning session of weights.

PREVENTING OVERTRAINING SYNDROME

Overtraining can have a dozen causes. Certainly, its effect can be devastating and can quickly end a swimmer's career. Early prevention is the most effective option. By the time symptoms of overtraining and persistent fatigue occur, repair is usually too late. As we have said, early dropout can be avoided, but it can seldom be cured. We have discussed a number of strategies aimed at early prevention. See the sidebar for an overview of some specific precautionary measures.

Treating swimmers as individuals is of the utmost importance. Each swimmer is different and has different tolerances to physical stress and responds differently to various training inputs. Custom and financial pressure lead many coaches to set training programmes that are the same for everyone. Other coaches train their best athlete, leaving everyone else to do the same schedule as best they can. However, achieving good performance from everyone requires dealing with each swimmer as an individual.

Overtraining and the resultant high and early dropout rate is a serious problem. It is ironic, therefore, that there is no single physiological test to identify the onset of the problem.

Two early warning protocols are recommended. First, the coaching environment should support self-analysis and discussion of stress-related issues. Factors should be discussed that include the athlete's perception of their training progress, their view of the programmed work load, their level of fatigue, their sleep quality and their muscle soreness. Second, the programme should include a regular evaluation of heart rate recovery through use of the Salo PulsePlot test.

PRECAUTIONARY MEASURES TO AVOID OVERTRAINING

1. Identify at-risk swimmers.

2. Reduce known causes, such as sudden changes in training stress, poor diet and excessive competition.

3. Take account of individual differences in personality and events.

4. Have a training programme that allocates distinct and separate periods to aerobic, anaerobic and speed training in a 40/20/40 balance.

5. Observe the hard day, easy day recovery rule, applying the principle of active rest and programming set holiday periods into the annual training plan.

6. Introduce a systematic coach and athlete evaluation protocol of the athlete's physical and mental condition.

7. Use monitoring sets such as the Salo PulsePlot.

CHAPTER 19

THE REST OF LIFE

Events that occur outside the pool can have a material effect on a swimmer's progress. Indeed, they can cause early teenage dropout. Many times, I have discussed the reasons for a swimmer deciding to quit. In almost every case issues outside of swimming have been included in the list of factors contributing to their decision.

There is not much a coach, or even parents, can do to prevent these outside forces. They are not right, they hurt and they should not occur. But I know of no way of preventing harm from outside. The best we can do is equip swimmers to handle the stress involved. In chapter 20, Jane describes her feelings as she flew out to begin a swimming scholarship in the United States. It is a dark essay – a depressing comment on the difficulties faced by a teenage swimmer in her quest to succeed. Jane was successful. Her coping mechanism worked, and she received four years of free education and swimming experience. She got a return, but there are many who do not. Here are some examples of what can go wrong.

My first story concerns Mohammed Ali who was flying into Miami Airport. The driver of his car called the airport to arrange to park Ali's car in a restricted zone that would allow the champion to get through the terminal quickly and avoid the pressing crowds that inevitably gathered when Ali appeared. According to plan, the driver parked in the restricted area and went into the airport to collect his employer. A few minutes later, they emerged to find a parking warden, standing at the car, writing a ticket. The chauffer explained that, because this was Mohammed Ali, the airport authorities had approved the arrangement. The warden was incensed – just because Ali was the world heavyweight boxing champion that did not give him the right to park anywhere he wanted – and defiantly stuck the ticket on the car window. The driver was about to argue when Ali gently put his hand on his shoulder and said, "Just take the ticket. It's more important to him than it is to us."

Now back to swimming: Several years ago, Rhi Jeffrey returned to Florida to train with our swim team. On her first afternoon, there was some excitement around the pool; an Olympic Gold medallist was about to join the squad. I was discussing the afternoon's training with Rhi when the pool manager came out of his office and strode purposely to where we were standing. "Has Rhi paid to get in to the pool?" he demanded.

"No" I said, "she is joining the swim team and the cost of her pool entry is covered in her coaching fees."

"I don't care about that," he said, "has she paid her coaching fees today?"

I explained that it was Rhi's first day back in Florida and her father, who lived in New York, would be paying the fees shortly. The pool manager, however, was not to be deterred. Either Rhi paid her training fees immediately or the cost of her pool entry was due. I paid him the $4. Clearly it meant more to him than it did to us.

Rhi wears a fun cap given to her by the team juniors. In this race she swam a long course personal best 100 meters fly in 1.01. Before the race she had to cut the small rubber fins off the top of cap. An official said they were a swimming aid.

Early in 2012, I heard that a New Zealand swimming official, Jo Davidson, had been appointed to work at the London Olympic Games. That news was beyond my comprehension. You see, back in the 2002 New Zealand summer championships, Jane was the favourite to win the 100-meter and 200-meter breaststroke. Shortly after the heat of the 200 meters, one of the lifeguards came to where I was sitting and said he thought I should know that he had just taken Jo Davidson and two referees down to the underwater viewing windows below the West Wave pool. As he let them in, he overheard Davidson tell the referees, "Now, Copland is swimming in the next heat, and I will show you what to disqualify her for in the final tonight."

It turns out the two referees were appointed to act in the finals session that night, and Jo Davidson was setting out to ensure a swimmer, whose father she didn't like, did not become a national champion. I went to the national coach, Clive Rushton, and asked him to deal with a rogue official. To his eternal credit, Clive took the complaint seriously and called for a hearing. Davidson looked extremely embarrassed, and well she should. That sort of behaviour has no place in any sport. Oh, and Jane was not disqualified and won the final.

A few years ago, a really good New Zealand swimmer, Emily Thomas, decided it was time to retire from swimming. I thought that was a shame. She was a good swimmer who had represented her country with distinction. Her bronze medal in the 50-meter backstroke at the Pan Pacific Games was New Zealand's best performance since the Jeffs, Simcic, Loader and Langrell era and was only matched recently by Lauren Boyle. What is inexcusable is that she left the sport without a mention by Swimming New Zealand. This athlete represented the sport of swimming in New Zealand with absolute commitment. The national federation had a duty to report and applaud her career. Ignoring her was inexcusable bad manners.

While I was coaching in the US Virgin Islands, I took the national team to Mexico City for the Central American and Caribbean Swimming Championships. One of our male swimmers got disqualified in the preliminaries of the 100-meter breaststroke. The disqualification slip had the previous year's date, the rule violation referred to butterfly, not breaststroke, and it had not been signed by either the turns judge or the referee. I decided to lodge a protest. At the hearing, I explained my confusion and asked for the swimmer to be reinstated. The referee was furious. He banged his fist down on the table and exclaimed that, had I been a lawyer, I was just the sort of person who got rapists off on a technicality. Really, I thought? Are you serious? The comparison with rape was unnecessary, and the swimmer was reinstated.

My next example also involves Jane. When she won her first New Zealand Open Short Course Championship, Jane swam most of her training at the Onekawa Pool in Napier, New Zealand. The pool manager decided Jane's swim deserved some recognition and posted her framed photograph on the wall in the pool reception area. The next day, at 6:00am, I noticed the mother of a girl who swam against Jane leaning forward, almost covering Jane's photograph and then quickly turn and walk out the door. I was suspicious and went to the reception area to check, and sure enough the frame was still on the wall, but the photograph had gone. I walked outside to see if the mother was still around. She wasn't, but what I did find was Jane's photograph in a garbage bin at the pool door. To this day I think the most horrifying sight I have seen in sport is the gouged fingernail marks down the side of Jane's face as the mother clawed the photograph out of its frame.

My final example involves money. This can be especially troubling for swimmers who have left home and are swimming a full senior programme but are not yet good enough to receive any state aid or commercial sponsorship. A senior swimming schedule makes it virtually impossible to work in full-time paid employment. Swimmers need to make ends meet financially with part-time work or assistance from home. Some swimmers have huge financial problems – unable to pay rent or their telephone account or buy petrol to get to the pool. Only the most determined survive. Many just give up the struggle, retire from swimming and begin a "normal" life. There is not much anyone can do about the financial cost of being a swimmer, but it is a problem that can make a long-term commitment to swimming very difficult indeed.

So Mohammed Ali was right. The bad behaviour of a parking warden, the Florida pool manager, mothers with an axe to grind, Jo Davidson and the national federation are best ignored. Ali's ability to turn the other cheek is the correct response and is a defense mechanism that needs to be learned by every ambitious swimmer.

Many squads ask swimmers to keep a diary of their training distances and timed swims. I have encouraged athletes struggling with problems outside swimming to include these factors in their training diary. The process of writing them down can bring order to chaos and often suggests a solution. If all that self-reporting achieves is to clear the mind, it is worthwhile. Certainly, high self-reported stress levels often herald the onset of symptoms of overtraining, even when the cause of the stress is not directly related to their sport. In the study conducted by Laurel MacKinnon, it was found that after six months of training, senior swimmers displayed high emotional stress levels four to six weeks before physical overtraining symptoms appeared and before their training or competition results declined. Self-reported stress, in other words, can be the earliest indicator of potential problems. Corrective action taken at this stage could avoid more serious issues and longer more disruptive intervention later.

In summary, swimmers can experience outside stress caused by finances, paid employment, school, time management and relationships with sport's officials, family and friends. Any of those can affect and can be aggravated by the further stress of training four to six hours a day. Laurel MacKinnon's study indicated that high self-reported stress levels are probably the earliest indicator of overtraining problems. The next chapter provides an insight into just how dark that world of athletic stress can become.

CHAPTER 20

THE DAMAGE ABUSE CAN DO

By Jane Copland Pavlovich

I wrote the following story at age 18, shortly after I left Napier for the United States. I don't identify with it at all anymore, 15 years later; in fact, I find it shockingly bitter and raw. That said, I remember feeling that bitter and raw, and I remember writing it and meaning every word. While I was fortunate to be cared for by a good coaching system and supportive family, some of the harassment my teammates and I suffered from the swimming establishment in our town were wholly unacceptable.

It defies belief that adult sports administrators and parents inflict vindictive abuse on children and young adults in their sport, especially given how common this apparently is; parental and administrative politics is infamous enough to be somewhat of a cliché in a handful of sports, including soccer, swimming and ballet among others. It should be said that this is completely different to receiving constructive criticism or having your coach's methods critiqued; grave issues arise when the abuse towards young athletes becomes vitriolic and personal. Along with establishing safe, nurturing training practices for fostering young talent, it is absolutely critical that abusive behaviour towards athletes be forcefully stamped out. No one should leave high school or youth swimming for college feeling as bitter as I did, especially not as a result of petty sports club politics and local administration's unwillingness to sanction bullying from their adult members. Unfortunately, this is a significant problem in youth sport.

THE LAST LITTLE AEROPLANE

Those small aeroplanes that fly from little towns all over the country only go to a few places, mostly Auckland and Wellington, and they rattle and bang as they hurtle down runways, past small brown seventies control towers and car parks full of 1992 Mazdas and SUVs, to wobble into the air like baby elephants standing up for the first time.

There was such a big earthquake here that a huge hill rose out of the ground and an island turned into a suburb where children play soccer on Saturday mornings. Rich people built their houses on the hill and parked their SUVs in the driveways so they could take their children to the island on Saturday mornings. Every week in the free newspaper that comes to the houses on and off the hill, centurions tell the story of the day the island became a suburb where people take their children to play soccer; how their classrooms heaved and swelled and the wooden buildings screamed and twisted and fell to the ground or were burnt. The place was in ruins, so they rebuilt it, street by street, from the trees beside the river to the Big Fresh, at the bottom of the new hill.

Years later, around the time the little rumbling, squeaking aeroplanes were made, they built an airport. Inside a little aeroplane, above the river and the hills and swamps, bastardised by earthquakes and Transit New Zealand projects, you can see all the SUVs and Mazdas going nowhere, from the island to the hill and back again.

Near the island there is a water park where they have strung lane ropes over the swimming pools and specified who can swim in them. The people with the Mazdas and SUVs take a detour in the mornings at six a.m. and go up and down in the lanes in the swimming pools. When it was near the day when the last little aeroplane would take off past the old brown control tower, I would hate all the people in the lanes in the swimming pools, and they would hate me, and I would think about when the last little aeroplane would take off at eleven in the morning in three hundred and sixty five days. How many hours was that? How many hours was that at the swimming pool, trying to be good and quiet and inconspicuous in the lanes? Trying to be invisible and unnoticed and to excel and grow to be eight feet tall at the same time?

There were some cold mornings when the ice was still caked to the car after two hours in the pool. I wondered why people got out of bed at six a.m. and drove their Mazdas and SUVs to the car park beside the swimming pool? I started computing how many lengths I would have to swim until I could be shaken around by the last little aeroplane.

One day the people who owned the Mazdas and the SUVs decided that I should not come to their swimming pool anymore and swim between their plastic lane ropes, so I went to a different place where the roof leaked and the water was cloudy and smelled strange, and it was hard to breathe at night because there was chlorine in my lungs. Someone there didn't think I should swim between their lane ropes, either, but there was nothing they could do about it because I made sure that I didn't do anything wrong. I didn't do anything, just swam up and down and tried to be good and quiet, but inside I was angry, and every night in bed I coughed chlorine and squirmed in my dry, burnt skin and thought of the last little aeroplane shuddering down the runway, and how you could never tell if there was an earthquake as you hurtled past the control tower and the car park.

I thought of the times I had swum in pools, between plastic lane ropes, wearing their uniform, showing the Aucklanders and the Wellingtonians how special we could be, even though we came from the town with the uprooted hill and pretend-island, and when I won they still sent me back to the cloudy, leaky swimming pool and they longed for the last little aeroplane, too.

I lived on the flat there. I couldn't see anything past the end of the road or the back fence of the car park. Once, I had lived so high on a hill that had it not been for the mountain on the other side of the valley, I could have seen forever. It was too calm here; the stubborn blue sky shows me the dire awfulness of my situation – just blue sky forever, not even a cloud. Sometimes it rained and the rain came straight down, as if the sky was bored. Nothing ever happened.

The blue serenity still remains and it quietly assumes it won because I went somewhere else, off to Auckland and then to heaven knows where, it doesn't matter, they don't think about what happens past the island and the hill and the car park, but she's not here anymore, the lanes of the pool are free for the nice people who get out of bed on the silent, tranquil, freezing, boring, dark mornings and she was last seen on one of the little aeroplanes that went trundling past the control tower in the morning, the date forgotten, but it was a while ago now.

When I see the foreign, exciting lights from the window, thousands of feet below, I wonder if you will think of me. Does it hurt that I never have to see your face again? It never made sense, just what you were trying to do to me. I know you will miss me; I know you will wish I was still there; the serenity will get to you all. One day the earthquake will shake your little serene Hell again and your hill will sink back into the sea, your island will be an island again and the world from my eyes will be balanced again. That is just the way nature works.

CHAPTER 21

RETIREMENT

Throughout this book we have discussed the chronic swimming problem of early teenage dropout. We have looked at the factors likely to cause dropout and identified ways of detecting early warnings that dropout might be about to happen. Finally, we have suggested remedial measures that can be taken to avoid the factors that cause young swimmers to leave the sport.

However, eventually everyone does retire. Some continue on as masters swimmers and others hang up their suits and never come under starter's orders again. At whatever stage a swimmer decides to retire, it is a big event. Any activity that has occupied up to five hours a day, six or seven days a week, for ten years or more, is going to end up leaving a void to be filled. Swimming will have brought marvellous highs, intense satisfaction and amazing fun. Swimming will have also been responsible for some bitter lows, some sadness and heartbreak. No activity that has gone on for so long and been so intrusive in the participant's life can be left with only a shrug and a, "Who cares?" Most swimmers need a coping mechanism in place to ease them through the transition into "civilian" life.

Here is an essay written by Jane with her thoughts on retirement from swimming.

I WAS ALMOST A TEENAGE DROPOUT

By Jane Copland Pavlovich

When you are growing up around a sport like swimming, you hear a lot of talk about "making it", but "it" is not usually well-defined. In fact, "it" is usually not defined at all. I've long been of the belief that no one really knows what "it" is. Sometimes, it refers to achieving a qualifying time or being accepted to a squad or programme, but it's often an arbitrary metric used to judge whether a young athlete has achieved as much as an observer thinks they should have.

For the purposes of this book, "it" could be said as satisfaction. "It" is the level at which the athlete is happiest with his or her achievements. "It" is knowing that you worked to the best of your abilities – both mental and physical – and reaped rewards to which you were entitled. Some people "make it" by qualifying for a small country's national championship. For others, "making it" is an Olympic medal.

It is not leaving the sport burnt out, tired, disappointed or frustrated. Certainly, many of us retire with small doubts about whether we could have been a little faster, timed a racing peak a little better, been a little more composed before a big race; however, an overall sense of satisfaction is rarely dampened more than a little bit by memories of things that could have gone a little bit better.

Given my level of talent, personal circumstances and abilities, I count myself as having "made it". I was recruited to several US universities, and I chose Washington State University in Pullman, Washington. By the time I arrived at WSU, I was New Zealand open women's short course 200-meter breaststroke record holder. I swam for WSU for four years, made it to NCAAs during my senior year and helped set a school record in the 800 freestyle relay (breaststroke was my mainstay, but I was useful in IMs and free races, too). When I retired, I was largely delighted with the whole experience. College had been a blast. There had been some hard times (my sophomore year was a big struggle), but I had made progress in all my events, travelled the United States, achieved a degree with honours and had what I still consider the experience of a lifetime. Swimming at NCAAs was most certainly the icing on a very satisfying cake. Although I didn't swim a personal best at NCAAs (my PB was and still is my qualifying swim), it was a good reward for 12 years of work.

For some people, that reward is a successful trip to the Olympics and for others, it's making a B final in a regional meet they never thought they would qualify for. But all of us who have been fortunate enough to know the feeling of "this is me at my best" can be said to have "made it". The aim of this book is to propel more young people to achieving happiness and satisfaction with their swimming.

Jane swimming the breaststroke

The closest I ever came to being a teenage dropout was during an afternoon training session in Napier, New Zealand, one hot Saturday afternoon when I was 16. As mentioned at various points throughout this book, my training situation in Napier wasn't good. We had no designated lane space (we couldn't have afforded it and would have been denied it even if we had had the money), so we swam in public lanes. If an event was taking place where public swimming was limited, then so were we. On this particular afternoon, after having swum a 10,000-meter session in the morning, my tiny squad and I were relegated to the aquatic complex's older swimming pool due to a water polo competition in our regular area.

The pool was too hot. It was overcrowded. The lane ropes weren't adequate, and they were never tight enough, meaning lanes were usually out of alignment and the water was wavy and rough. We were sharing a 25-meter lane with two or three irritated members of the public. Every length swum was a jostling, hot, wavy mess. On top of that, we were the black sheep of the area's swimming scene, and I was acutely aware that any visible frustration or anger from me would be immediately reported to pool management and sanctioned. No matter how many elbows I took to the ribs and how many 45-year-old men pushed off directly in front of me and moved out to not let me pass, I had to keep my temper.

To compound all this, it wasn't as if this were a one-off event. Every other day, training was interrupted or underscored by disruption or conflict that I made every effort at avoiding. This took a lot of emotional energy which, as described previously, can lead directly to burnout and the inability of an athlete to continue. The only positive, solid stable part of my swimming were the sessions David wrote and helped me execute. The training saved me.

In between sets, the three or four of us swimming together that afternoon were standing at the wall. David was on the side of the pool, speaking to one of my squad mates. I had zoned out and was absolutely overcome, suddenly and almost unshakably, with the feeling that I did not want to do this anymore – 10,000 meters in the morning, 5,000 more this afternoon in a hot, wavy bathtub where an exasperated sigh in the wrong direction would have a lifeguard threaten me with expulsion from the complex for bad behaviour. I was 16. My friends dedicated their lives to school and a burgeoning interest in parties, alcohol and boys. I had enjoyed some modest successes as an age group swimmer, and the idea of going to the United States for university had already been floated, but that was over two years away, and I had to improve substantially before a good college would look my way. I could barely find the stomach to put up with two more minutes in that pool, let alone two more years.

David's discussion with the other swimmer continued, and I could feel the words sitting in my mouth. I quit, I want to stop, I want to go home, I don't want to do this anymore. They were as real as if I had actually said them, blurting them out to interrupt David and the other athlete.

Why I swallowed those words and faced down that pool for another set, however many more thousand meters and the same again the next day for two more years, I wouldn't have been able to tell you at the time. Maybe I was partially saved by a strangely positive mirror of "sunk cost fallacy", where people continue doing something simply because they feel they have invested a lot into it already in spite of evidence that they should quit. Fortunately for me, my investment had not actually sunk, and I reaped its rewards in the end, but I wasn't to know that at 16. However, the dreadful feeling that I was young, burned out, wasted and upset and just wanted it to stop never afflicted me again. There were plenty of bad sessions and races after that, but I had the resolve to keep going with a largely positive outlook. The methods described in this book are a big part of why I was able to fight off an almost nauseous wave of desire to quit. And knowing the desperation to rid myself of a pretty unhappy existence in sport, I am interested in helping steer young swimmers and coaches away from mistakes that result in misery and early retirement.

A TEENAGER'S PERSPECTIVE

For adults it's somewhat confusing why young swimmers find it hard to grasp that just a year or two more in their current situation is all it takes to get a college scholarship or otherwise graduate to senior ranks. When we think about doing something we claim to love for two years to get a massive reward, the notion doesn't seem bad. Many of us have worked at jobs we don't like very much in order to progress, receive pay raises and promotions, or add to our resumes in search of something better. This is all but expected.

However, for a 16-year-old, two years is a different timeframe than it is for an adult. When I was 16 and desperate for the nightmarish swimming pool situation to end, my frame of reference for "only two more years" was that two years ago, I had been 14 and not much more than a child. If forever and eternity had been baked together and spat out in calendar format, they would still be less than the time it would take me to get from Onekawa's hot, hostile swimming pool and to the United States. This difference in perspective needs to be kept in mind when planning for and encouraging young swimmers.

Expecting young adults to sacrifice the lifestyles enjoyed by their non-athlete peers with the promise of better spoils later on is a similar exercise, but is a lot more complicated and difficult to quantify. Like for like, a teenage swimmer could be said to forego weekend sleep-ins, local parties and part-time jobs for international travel, national representation and – most importantly – personal success after years of hard work. The money earned from a part-time job would pale in comparison to a good college scholarship. The celebration after the biggest success of your career would put regular teenage parties to shame. But not only is this very hard to envision in the midst of difficult physical and mental training, it's also not a given consequence of that training; we are all aware, even as quite young swimmers, that some people's hard work doesn't pay off in the ways they hoped or expected. As such, we're giving up some of the primary parts of teenage life for a much harder existence, and a big fat "maybe" when it comes to our potential rewards. Clearly, if the methods described in this book are adhered to, a young person has a much greater chance of achieving the standards of which he or she is capable. However, thoughts of "why am I really missing out on all that?" still plague the mind of a teenager who has dedicated their life to something like swimming.

Eudaimonic well-being refers to the sense of fulfilment or "happiness" a person gets from being involved in or having completed something of meaning. It's an Aristotelian concept, but it doesn't take any knowledge of philosophy to understand or relate to: a child who has learned to button her shirt without help feels joy as a result, but that feeling is different to the joy the same child feels from having eaten a tasty ice cream.

What we're doing when we give up the pleasures of teenage parties and sleeping in every weekend is giving up hedonic pleasures for eudaimonic ones. Unsurprisingly, eudaimonia is considered a higher level of self-satisfaction and enjoyment that hedonism (and this is certainly a simplification of the theories, but it works when modelling the difficulties of pursuing this lifestyle at a young age). Young swimmers understand and crave the feelings of success that come with achievements in swimming; at the same time, it is hard work, day after day, year after year, to very infrequently indulge in an ice cream cone in favour of successfully doing up your buttons.

It's worth asking swimmers who did progress past the age of 18 and into senior ranks what they think differentiated them from their peers who quit. As is pointed out throughout this book, the defining characteristic of those who were successful is not necessarily measured in their speed or achievements when compared to others in the pool. Conversely, success isn't solely measured by simply having lasted longer than other people: for the purposes of "surviving junior swimming", a person should have completed a fulfilling swimming career that saw them explore their potential and retire on a largely positive note.

Posing the question of what they thought kept them in the sport through their teenage years and into college, several NCAA Division I swimmers provided us with a variety of answers that speak to similar themes. More than once, the swimmers mentioned swimming being an outlet for them, a "mental break" from everything else that went on in their lives. This sentiment seems almost incidental on the surface, but it is actually extremely important: despite the challenges swimming presents, training was often a source of relief and pause from other pressures. Even when they were training hard, the sport brought an element of calm to their lives. Abused athletes suffering from burnout are highly unlikely to echo this sentiment.

Secondly, several swimmers mentioned that swimming was something they were proud of. One said it made her feel "like a badass". These are inherently positive sentiments. On the opposite end of the spectrum, swimmers who mentioned when they "nearly" quit cite bad coaches as a primary reason and different good coaches as a reason they were drawn back to the sport. A swimmer who quit in high school but decided to take the sport up again at the collegiate level after trialling with the team mentions her gratitude to the coaches who took a chance on her and helped her succeed, while another athlete mentions a "non-swim coach" who told her she "wasn't Division I quality". (Clearly she was, as she swam in a Division I programme for the entirely of her college career and made significant progress.)

It's extremely unsettling to realise how many coaches interact with young people on a daily basis who are comfortable saying things like "you are not Division I quality". Good coaches don't say these things, no matter what they believe about the talent and prospects of an athlete. This is not to say that good coaches give athletes a false sense of what they can achieve: telling a swimmer with a modest amount of talent that he or she will be able to swim in the Olympic Games is not helpful. A good coach shows a person what they can expect from their careers and lays out a positive, achievable plan to work towards those goals. If a coach fully believes that the athlete can't achieve a certain standard, there is still no need or excuse for condescending negativity. Instead, the coach should suggest a workable roadmap for achieving the levels of success of which the athlete is capable. Despite the incorrect assessment, imagine if the coach in the previous example had said instead, "You plan on studying exercise science, right? This Division II college in Oregon has a great programme and a wonderful swim team. I think you'd fit in and really enjoy yourself."

KNOWING WHEN TO RETIRE

Being a sport that people often take up in childhood, swimming can be so ingrained in a person's sense of self that the idea of quitting is frightening. For many of us, our identities are interwoven with the sport. Who are we without swimming? This coupling of our sense of self with our status as an athlete can make retirement all the more painful, especially if a person feels dissatisfied with the cumulation of his or her career. Add to this that many swimming environments breed a culture where people who quit are looked down upon, and the end of many young people's careers are a lot harder for them to handle and result in a lot more bitterness.

As a teenager, an insult to my swimming felt like a strike right at the heart of who I was. I'm not unique in this sense either as the sentiment is fairly common. However, I was lucky enough to arrive at the end of my college career on a high note and one I could identify as about the peak of my ability (not to mention the looming necessity to get a job and join the working world). I qualified for the NCAA Championships in the 200 breaststroke and travelled down to Athens, Georgia, to compete as one of only two swimmers from my university. Swimming at NCAAs had been a goal since my freshman year, where I had missed out by 0.07 in the 200 breaststroke, and I had been off the pace by a larger margin in my sophomore and junior years. A week before I went to college, I'd expressed the excitement I felt about potentially competing at the NCAA Championships to a fellow swimmer in New Zealand. "Well," she'd said. "That's if you make it."

Finally, I had made it. However, reaching the pinnacle of my physical ability and after over 10 years of taking myself seriously as a swimmer, I'd had enough.

This makes me one of the lucky ones; not everybody finds a peaceful pinnacle. Someone burned out on years of anaerobic training whose results are plateauing before their time will have a far more difficult time making peace with letting that part of their identity go. As noted elsewhere in this book, the careers of burning-out and plateauing swimmers are salvageable by a caring, cautious enough coach. Rescuing a career about to end prematurely can be done. If you are a coach taking on a damaged swimmer who wants to give swimming another shot (one former NCAA athlete we spoke to returned to the sport during her freshman year of college with the help of compassionate coaches), care and caution are paramount to building a base of strength in the swimmer. Both their mental and physical strength may need significant attention to steer them away from a frustrating, premature retirement.

As has been noted recently by swimmers at the top of the sport like Katinka Hozzsu, swimming is not a sport that makes anyone any money besides those at its pinnacle, and even then, their incomes are not stable or guaranteed. Despite swimming demanding a level of dedication and professionalism that absolutely defies its amateur status, it's perfectly understandable for swimmers to put education or work commitments ahead of their sport as they get older. However, this is perhaps a question for a different book: the unfortunate circumstance of swimmers rarely training and competing at a high level once parental or college scholarship funding has dried up, despite being stronger physically and mentally than they were as children.

Finally, if you are coaching a swimmer who chooses to retire, the most important thing you can do is help the swimmer navigate their departure from the sport with positivity and dignity. Remember how close to our hearts swimming has been for us, often since we were young children and usually during some of the most formative times of our lives. Even somebody retiring on a very positive note will probably find the process an emotional one at best. Regularly, parents and coaches appear to misunderstand what they can realistically encourage a swimmer to do if the swimmer doesn't want to do it; swimming is too tough a sport to force participation and progress. A common misconception regarding my relationship with my father was that he must have "forced me" to swim, given that he was a professional coach and I was an athlete. On the contrary, no amount of outside pressure can get the best results out of someone who is not committed to the same goals. And if a swimmer comes to you with the resolve to retire, besides exploring how they came to that conclusion, that decision should be respected.

CREDITS

DESIGN & LAYOUT

Cover and
Interior Design: Annika Naas

Layout: www.satzstudio-hilger.de

Cover Photo: © AdobeStock

Interior Photos
and Illustrations: © David Wright, unless otherwise noted

EDITORIAL

Managing Editor: Elizabeth Evans